SHOOTING

Organized crime in photos

Dead Mobsters, Gangsters and Hoods.

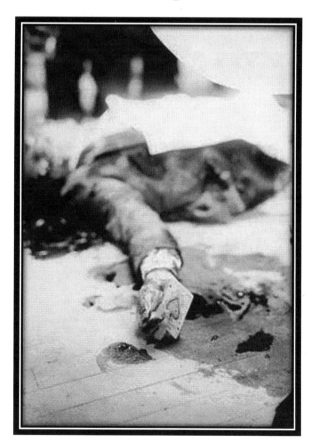

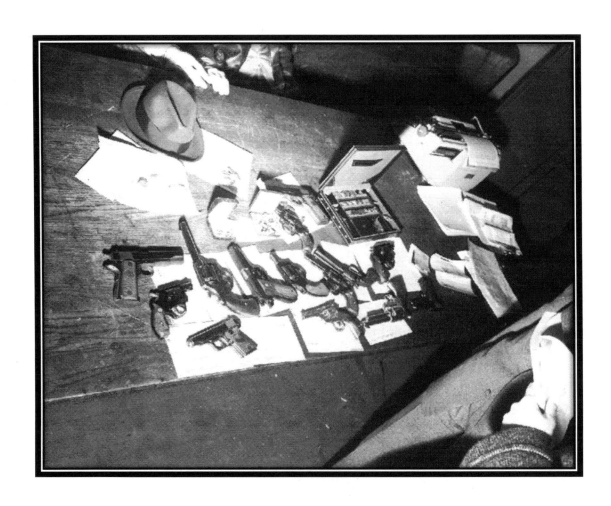

The Late Mr. Alterie

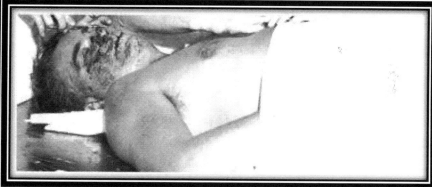

"Two Gun Louie" Alterie was born 1886. Died in Chicago July 18 1935, O'Bannion gang member, called Two Guns. Although he actually did carry two guns, both of the pearl handled pistols, the name was mostly used a form of ridicule against the colorful gangster. Murdered by the mob 1935 under orders of Frank Nitti after Alterie (Who claimed to have once been a member of the Denver Colorado Police) refused to give up his control of several local labor unions.

The Late Mr. Amberg

Louis Pretty Amberg

The Amberg brothers were Joseph Amberg (Born 1892, in Russia. Died September 30, 1935) and his brothers, Hyman (The Rat) Louis (Called Pretty because he was exceedingly ugly) and Oscar were vicious labor racketeering and other criminal activities in New York during the 1920s and 1930s. (The last brother, William, ran a furniture store in Brooklyn and had no criminal record)

The brother's primary rivals were the equally vicious Jacob "Gurrah" Shapiro, Louis "Lepke" Buchalter, Abe "Kid Twist" Reles and the Shapiro Brothers. The brothers were probably the first to charge 20% interest on their loans and fought for control of the Brownsville neighborhood in a partnership with Little Frank Teitelbaum.

Joey Amberg had 13 arrests on his record, starting in 1908 when he was jailed for burglary. He served five years in Sing-Sing Prison for assault and three years in federal prison for narcotics peddling.

Hymie Amberg committed suicide while jailed at the Tombs in 1926 while he awaiting trial for the murder of a Brooklyn jeweler named Aaron Rodack. Oscar Amberg, another brother, was charged with bringing the weapons that Hymie used trying to escape. Hyman managed to murder the warden and a guard, before taking his own life. Oscar was acquitted.

Joey Amberg made most of his living as a loan shark in Brooklyn Jewish community and he was widely hated. On September 30, 1935, at high noon, Joey Amberg and his driver Morris Kessler (Born 1892) were ambushed in garage at the corner of Blake and Christopher Avenue in Brownsville (Brooklyn) At the time Amberg lived at 190 East Seventeenth Street in Brooklyn (The property still stands. Kessler lived at 50 Tapscott Street in Brooklyn. Amberg parked his gray limousine at the garage and picked up each day to tour his rackets. As the pair stepped into the garage, (The place was massive and covered most of the block) three young men dressed in blue work clothes walked in and pulled out pistol from their coats. One of them said to Amberg "Back up Joe" when Amberg back up to the wall, one of the men said "Got you now Joe, how does it feel?" The gunmen then fired twelve shots into Amberg and Kessler, killing them both. Amberg was hit five times, mostly in the left lower back and left back of the head. Kessler, who turned to face the killers as he was shot, was hit four times, mostly in the face.

A month later, the remaining and eldest brother, Louis AKA Pretty (Born 1897) was found hacked to death near the Brooklyn Navy Yard on October 23, 1935 (the same day Dutch Schultz was murdered) at 1:15 in the morning. The insane killer Abe Reles said of Pretty Amberg "The word was that he was kinda nuts" And he was. Amberg's record, almost exclusively limited to assaults, started on November 3, 1914. In total he was arrested 15 times, and was found innocent for lack of evidence on virtually every charge. He was also the prime suspect in 18 murders. He was credited with inventing the so-called "Sack murder" in which the victim was tied with wire around the neck, arms and legs and eventually strangled themselves trying to escape. His hacked up, nude body was found inside a burning car at 131 North Elliot place in Brooklyn (The address no longer

5

exists). It was wrapped in blankets and tied around the ankles and wrists with wire. He had been cut up with an axe at least ten hours before. Amberg had spent the previous week at different Turkish bathes around the lower east side, probably as a means to protect himself.

Joey, Little Frank Teitelbaum and Louis were more than probably murdered by a cop killer named Albert Stern AKA The Teacher. (His real name was probably Stein, he was born 1914) Stern, a morphine addict, had once worked for the Amberg's, ended the relationship when he robbed Joey Amberg on his extortion money (it turned out to be less than $70) and then with other members of the gang broke off on his own and started to pull off kidnappings.

Convinced that the Amberg's and Teitelbaum would turn him into police for crimes of the past, Stern went on a murderous rampage and wiped the brothers out. Stein was found dead on October 27, 1935, hung by the neck, in a cheap New Jersey boarding house. It has never been established whether he killed himself or was murdered.

The late Mr. Anastasia

There was only one last thing in the way of Vito Genovese from taking over the organization that would one day take his name and that was Albert Anastasia. Back in the 1930's, when Lucky Luciano approached Anastasia about his plot to kill Joe the Boss Masseria and take over the mob, Anastasia, desperate for power, pushed Luciano to launch the plan. When it was successful, Luciano rewarded Anastasia for his loyalty by naming him under boss to the Mangano family under Vincent Mangano. However, in 1951, Anastasia grew tired of Mangano, and with Frank Costello's support, he had Mangano and his brother Phil shot to death and took over the family.

Carlo Gambino

So while Frank Costello might have accepted his fate at Genoese's hands, Anastasia didn't. Anastasia went to the Commission members and openly accused Genovese of an illegal hit on Costello, and he began to talk about going to war with Genovese, a war to reinstate Costello to power, a war that he would probably win. Then Genovese learned that Costello and Anastasia were meeting secretly, and he panicked. He would have to kill Anastasia, before Anastasia killed him, but he would need the permission of the national commission, the shot taken at Costello had taught him that much.

Getting the commission's permission wasn't difficult. For them, Anastasia had grown too ambitious and was talking about ruling over all of New York and Las Vegas, which is exactly what all the other bosses wanted but feared to try to do. Anastasia had no such fears. In fact, he had already made a grab at the narcotics and gambling cash that was flowing out of Havana's from Lansky's racket and into the pockets of various Mafia and syndicate bosses across the globe.

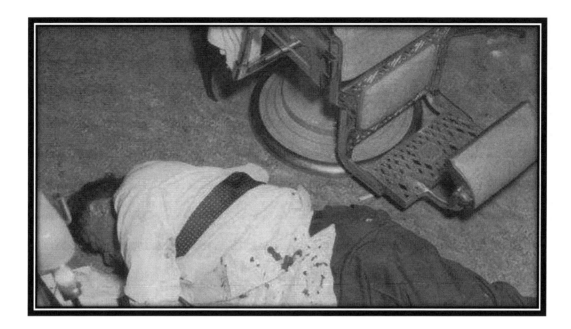

Anastasia's mistake was inviting Cuba's other crime boss, Santos Trafficante, to join him in his efforts to take over the underworld. Trafficante could hand Cuba over to Anastasia, without his having to go through Lansky and Alo, who may have already entered an agreement with Genovese. Trafficante heard Anastasia out and told he needed to think about his offer. Instead, to protect his own assets in Cuba, Trafficante went straight to Genovese and cut his own deal. In turn, Genovese, with Trafficante behind him, took Anastasia's plan to the national commission who sanctioned the hit.

Genovese contacted Carlo Gambino, the cunning and ambitious capo under Anastasia, and convinced him that they would both benefit by murdering Anastasia. Gambino agreed and set up the hit.

On October 25, 1957, the Gallo brothers killed Anastasia as he sat in the barbershop's chair at the Sheraton Hotel, a hot towel wrapped around his face. There were eleven people in the tiny shop, five barbers, a manicurist, three shoe shine boys and two customers who watched the two young hoods quickly enter the shop and put at least ten bullets into his head and neck.

There was no big dollar, flashy mobster funeral for Anastasia. In fact, the mob barely showed up at all. Instead, his family attended the simple ceremony. Anastasia's wife Elsa, who married him in 1937 at age nineteen always refused to believe that her husband was a Mafia killer. The Anastasia she knew never drank, was home by 9 p.m. and took the children to see movies "I never heard him say a bad word in front of me or the children. He never spoke roughly. He used to go to church with me every Sunday. He gave generously to the church... Now he's not even buried in consecrated ground."

The late Messrs. Anselmi, Scalise, Guinta

Albert Anselmi, John Scalise and Hop Toad Guinta

It was gangsters Albert Anselmi and John Scalise who introduced the idea to Chicago gangland that rubbing bullets in garlic would assure a kill, since the garlic would enter the blood system and finish the victim off if the gunshot didn't. Actually, rubbing the bullets in garlic only sterilized them. However, they did introduce the more successful "handshake kill" -- grasping a victim's hands in a welcome and then shooting his head off.

It worked on gang leader Dion O'Bannion and underworld financier Matt Kolb, although it was probably only Anselmi who took part in the Kolb killing, with Paul Ricca. Later, when Hymie Weiss offered to make peace with Capone if he would turn over O'Bannon's killers so he could murder them, Capone said, "Is he nuts? I wouldn't do that to a yellow dog." Actually Capone would have turned them over, but since Weiss was on the run anyway, and Anselmi and Scalise worked for so little money, Capone walked away from the offer. The day came when the Genna's ordered the pair to kill Al Capone, which they knew was suicide. So instead of killing Capone, they went to him with the plot and offered him their services to kill the Genna's instead.

Capone took them up on the offer. Anselmi and Scalise lured one Genna into a trap where he was killed, and killed another brother shortly afterward. Then Scalise and Anselmi turned on Capone. The pair entered into a plot by a pair of gunmen named Joe Giunta and Joey Aiello, to kill Capone.

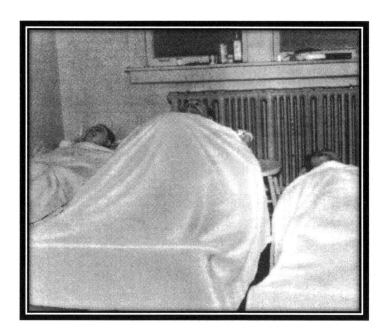

Frankie Rio, Capone's bodyguard, learned of the plot and told Capone about, it but Capone refused to believe that Scalise and Anselmi would sell him out.

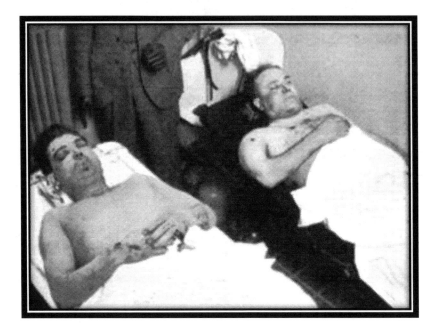

To prove it, he and Rio rigged a fake argument that ended with Rio slapping Capone across the face while Scalise and Anselmi watched. The next day, Scalise & Anselmi approached Rio and let him in on the plot to kill Capone. Rio took the information, with proof back to Capone. A week later, on May 7, 1929, Capone hosted a dinner in Scalise and Anselmi honor, at a casino called The Plantation, outside of Chicago.

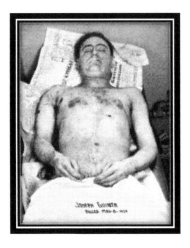

When the enormous formal dinner was ended, Capone stood and made a short speech on loyalty and then accused Scalise and Anselmi of plotting to kill him. Before Scalise or Anselmi could defend themselves, Capone pulled a Louisville slugger baseball bat out from under the table, and swung it down hard, first on Anselmi, who, according to witnesses, was still smiling when the first swing hit him in the skull, and then on Scalise, whose only words were, "Jesus, Mother of God Al, No! Please no!"

Their dead bodies were found along a roadside days later, bound in bailing wire, their eyes gone, not a bone in their bodies unbroken. They had been shot, by Jack McGurn, three times each, in the back of the head.

The late Mr. Anton

Teddy Anton

Teddy Anton was the Owner of the Anton Hotel, a long time personnel friend of Capone's, he disappeared presumed murdered 1925 by Al Capone for reasons unknown, although its speculated that Capone, in a drunken rage, beat the tavern owner to death.

The late Mr. Barker

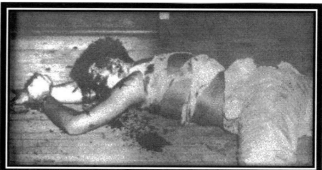

Freddie Barker, Ma Barkers boy

On January 16, 1935, Ma Barker and her son Fred were gunned down in a rented house home on Lake Weir, Florida. When agents with the Department of Justice, now called the Federal Bureau of Investigation, arrived at the Ocklawaha rental home that morning, 63-year-old Ma opened the front door. Seconds later, 32-year-old Fred walked onto the porch and unloaded a volley of machine gun bullets on the government agents. For the next four or five hours, the two sides exchanged gunfire almost continuously.

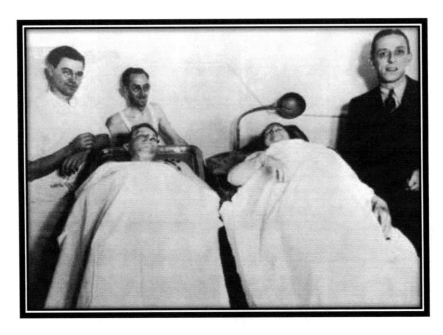

Freddie and Ma Barker, dead

Finally about noon, about an hour after the shooting from inside the home stopped, agents sent Willie Woodberry -- who had been hired by the Barkers to cook -- into the home. As Woodberry walked onto the porch, he yelled, "It's me Ma, don't shoot." Ma and Fred were dead. The house was riddled with nearly 3,500 bullets in the shootout

The Barrel Murders

In April of 1903, police discovered the body of Benditto Madonia stuffed into a barrel at Ave. A and 11th St. The corpse had 18 stab wounds; the throat had been slit; the penis and testicles had been shoved into his mouth, suggesting that he had been a police informer. The throat was cut from ear to ear, the head almost severed from eighteen stab wounds in the neck.

The body had been forcibly pushed into the barrel with the head resting between the knees. The coroner concluded that stab wounds to the neck were inflicted before the killing cut to the jugular vein, this meant he was either attacked in his sleep or restrained as he was tortured. In his pocket was a piece of paper, upon which was written 'Come at Once!' in Italian. Madonia's body could have been tossed into the East River, quietly, but it wasn't, the killers wanted it to be discovered, they wanted to send a message.

The Late Mr. Bennet

Billy Bennett

Billy Bennett was part of Boston's mostly Irish Charlestown Mob was that was led by the McLaughlin Brothers (Bernie, Georgie, and Edward "Punchy" McLaughlin) and their associates, brothers Stevie and Connie Hughes from Charlestown. The Bennett boys, Billy and Eddie were long time members of the organization. The gang fought the Somerville's Winter Hill Gang led by James "Buddy" McLean in a decade long war in the 1960's, (1961-167) which is where Billy Bennett caught his. The spart that started the war came on Labor Day weekend 1961 when Georgie McLaughlin made an advance on the girlfriend of Winter Hill Gang member Alex Rocco, who later had a starring role in The

Godfather as Moe Greene. Winter Hill gangsters beat McLaughlin badly enough to send him to the hospital. Bernie McLaughlin demanded that the men who beat his brother be handed over to him. When the Winter Hills refused, the McLaughlin's attempted to wire a bomb to McLean's wife's car. In retaliation, McLean shot and killed Bernie McLaughlin coming out of the "Morning Glory" bar in Charlestown, Massachusetts in October 1961. This was the start of Boston's Irish Gang War.

The late Mr. Bilotti

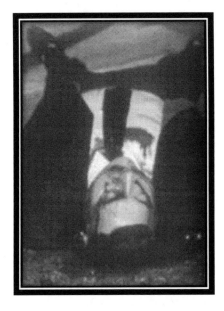

Just about everyone in the Gambino crime family hated Paul Castellano's underboss Tommy Bilotti so on December 16, 1985 when the time came for John Gotti and his drug dealing arm of the family to get rid of Castellano they didn't hesitate to take out Bilotti with him when the pair pulled up in front of Manhattan's Sparks Steak House in Manhattan.

The late Mr. Binaggio

Charles Binaggio Charles Binaggio was boss of the Kansas City crime family. On the night of April 6, 1950, Binaggio and his underboss, Charles "Mad Dog" Gargotta, were called to meet someone, no one knows who it was for sure, at the First Ward Democratic Club near downtown Kansas City. Binaggio left his driver/bodyguard, Nick Penna, at a mob owned tavern, saying that he would return in a few minutes.

Binaggio and Gargotta then borrowed a car and drove off to the Democratic Club. Shortly after 8:00 PM , residents in apartments above the Democratic Club heard several shots. Eight hours later, a cab driver going to a nearby cafe noticed that the club door was open; he also heard water running inside. The police were called and they found Binaggio and Gargotta inside the club. Binaggio was seated at a desk and Gargotta was lying inside the front door. Both men had been shot in the head four times with separate .32 caliber revolvers. The police theorized that Gargotta had been trying to escape the club when he was shot in the back of the head.

The late Mr. Birns

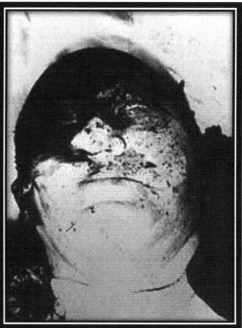

Alex Birns AKA Shondor was a Cleveland mobster who was once labeled as the city's Public Enemy No. 1 by the local newspapers. In March 1975, Birns was blown up via a bomb containing C-4, a potent military explosive in the lot behind Christy's Lounge, a go-go spot at 2516 Detroit Ave. Birns was blown several feet through the roof of the car and his torso landed near the passenger door.

Birns was still alive, though barely. A passerby managed to drag away Birns's upper torso since Birns had been blown in half. His face, arms and chest were bloodied and blackened. Birns's nose was broken when his body landed on the street after being blown out the top of his car. His hair was scorched off from the heat of the horrific blast. His severed legs landed fifty feet away and other smaller parts of him were scattered all over the place. Towards his death, the upper part of his body was convulsing violently. A chain link fence between Christy's and St. Malachi Church caught many of the smaller fragments of flesh and bone. Police suspected Irish gangster Danny Greene as well as a gang of Black numbers runners in the killing.

The late Mr. Bolles

Bolles car after the bombing

On June 2, 1976, investigative reporter Don Bolles left behind a short note in his office typewriter explaining he would meet with an informant, then go to a luncheon meeting, and be back about 1:30 p.m. The source promised information on a land deal involving top state politicians and possibly the mob. A wait of several minutes in the lobby of the Hotel Clarendon was concluded with a call for Bolles himself to the front desk, where the conversation lasted no more than two minutes. Bolles then exited the hotel, his car in the adjacent parking lot just south of the hotel on Fourth Avenue.

Apparently, Bolles started the car, even moving a few feet, before a remote detonated bomb consisting of six sticks of dynamite taped to the underside of the car beneath the driver's seat was detonated, the impact shattering his lower body, opening the driver's door, and leaving him mortally wounded while half outside the vehicle. Both legs and one arm were amputated over a ten day stay in St. Joseph's Hospital; the eleventh day was the reporter's last. However, his last words after being found in the parking lot the day of the bombing were: "They finally got me. The Mafia. Emprise. Find John (Harvey Adamson)."

The exact motive for the crime remains a mystery, but many speculate the Mafia holds responsibility, as a large concentration of Bolles' work involved organized crime, even going as far as to run a story naming over 200 known mafia members operating in the state of Arizona.

The late Mr. Bontade

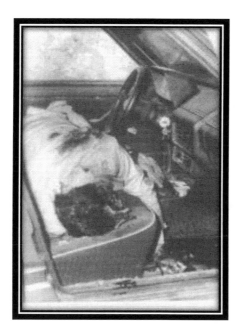

Stefano Bontade was an extremely powerful boss of Santa Maria di Gesù family in Corleone Italy until he was shot to death on April 23, 1981. His killing began the most violent mafia war in the history which in the 1981-83 period left more than 1.000 dead.

The late Mr. Borsellino

On July 19th 1992, Italian judge Paolo Borsellino, who was investigating the Mafia, was killed a bomb-car put in Palermo. Killed with him were policemen Agostino Catalano, Vincenzo Li Muli, Walter Cosina, Claudio Traina and Emanuela Loi.

The late Mr. Brooks

Chicago Bootleggers Dynamite Joe Brooks and Eddie Harmening. Both men were probably killed for their failed attempt on the life his boss Joe Saltis. Although others blame the murder on inter-gang disputes.

The late Mr. Buchalter

Louis "Lepke" Buchalter was head of the Mafia hit squad Murder, Inc. during the 1930s. In 1936, Murder Inc. killers, acting on Buchalter's orders, gunned down a Brooklyn businessman named Joseph Rosen. Rosen was a former garment industry trucker whose union Buchalter took over in exchange for ownership of a Sutter Avenue candy store. Rosen had aroused Buchalter's ire by failing to heed warnings to leave town. Although no proof exists that Rosen was cooperating with the District Attorney, Buchalter nevertheless believed it to be true. Buchalter became the only major mob boss to have received the death penalty in the United States after being convicted of that murder.

Buchalter's order for the Rosen hit had been overheard by Abe Reles, who turned state's evidence in 1940 and fingered Buchalter for four murders.

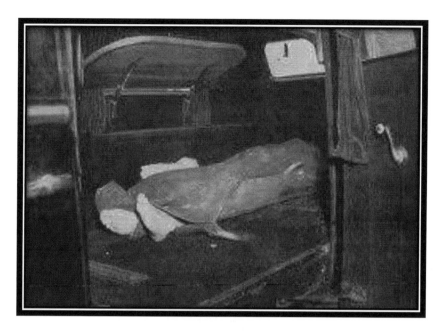

Buchalter, dead.

Four hours after they were handed the case, the jury arrived at a verdict at 2 am on 30 November 1941, finding Buchalter guilty of first degree murder, the penalty for which was death by electrocution. Also convicted and sentenced to death for the same crime were two of Buchalter's lieutenants who had participated in the planning and commission of the Rosen murder, Emanuel "Mendy" Weiss, and Louis Capone.

After his last appeal for mercy was rejected, Louis Buchalter was executed on Saturday, March 4, 1944 on the electric chair in Sing Sing. On the same day, a few minutes before Buchalter's execution, his lieutenants Weiss and Capone were also executed.

The Late Mr. Bruno

Angelo "The Gentle Don" Bruno (born Angelo Annaloro) ran the Philadelphia crime family for two decades. Bruno gained his nickname and reputation due to his preference for conciliation over violence.

Several factions within the Philadelphia family began conspiring to betray the aging Bruno. On March 21, 1980, the 69 year-old Bruno was killed by a shotgun blast in the back of the head as he sat in his car. It is believed that the killing was ordered by Antonio Caponigro (aka Tony Bananas), Bruno's consigliere. A few weeks later, Caponigro's body was found stuffed in a body bag in the trunk of a car in New York City. About $300 in bills were jammed in his mouth and anus (to be interpreted as signs of greed). The Commission had reportedly ordered Caponigro's murder because he assassinated Bruno without their sanction. Other Philadelphia family members involved in Bruno's murder were tortured and killed.

After Caponigro's murder, Philip 'Chicken Man' Testa led the family for one year until he was killed by a nail bomb at his home. Testa's death resulted from an attempt by Peter Casella, Testa's underboss, and Frank "Chickie" Narducci, a capo, to become the Philadelphia boss and underboss. After Testa's death, Scarfo took over the Philadelphia family. In the ensuing years, the Philadelphia family would be decimated by government informants, more infighting, and the prosecutions of Scarfo and other mobsters.

The late Mr. Cagnoni

Michael Cagnoni's cars after the explosion

Mike Cagnoni was an otherwise legitimate trucking executive who was murdered by Chicago hood Frankie Calabrese Sr. on June 24, 1981 in DuPage County, Illinois. Cagnoni was killed because mob boss Joe Ferriola wanted to take over Cagnoni's trucking business. Calabrese testified that he and his crew began following Cagnoni to determine his routine, which proved nearly impossible. So they used a remote-control bomb that was placed under the front seat of Cagnoni's green Mercedes-Benz.

The plan was to detonate the bomb as Cagnoni drove on an expressway. But the day of the bombing, Cagnoni's wife took the car to drive their son to school and headed in a direction away from the detonator and was saved. "This poor woman got in the car," Nicholas said. "If she had come east, not west...." His voice trailed off and he paused, showing his first expression of concern. "I don't know what I felt." The plan to kill Cagnoni was foiled several times. In the first attempt, the bomb under his seat didn't detonate. The crew members had to determine how big of an antenna would be needed to set off a bomb. They even went as far to get an exact model of Cagnoni's car to practice unlocking the door, Nicholas said.

The late Mr. Canavan

Myles Canavan ran a large Chicago gambling ring and was costing Al Capone money. The mob sent out feelers to try and bring the Irishman into the Capone flock. When that failed, they killed him in the parking lot of his luxury apartment house and took over his operations.

The late Mr. Capone

 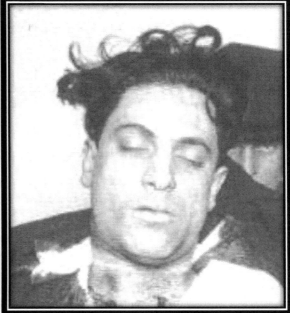

Frank Capone

In 1923, Chicago voters elected a new mayor, William Dever, who proceeded to crack down on Torrio, the Capone brothers, and their South Side Gang. In response, Torrio tasked Al with creating speakeasies, brothels, and illegal gambling dens in Cicero, a Chicago suburb. Within a year, Al Capone had placed the Cicero city manager Joseph Z. Klenha and the town committeemen on the gang payroll. Frank Capone, Al's brother, was given the job to represent the gang in its dealings with the Cicero town council. Frank was mild mannered compared to his brother Al, projecting the image of a respectable businessman, always attired in a neat suit.

In the April 1, 1924, primary election, Democratic Party politicians mounted a serious election challenge to Republican Klenha and his associates. To protect the gang's political control of Cicero, Frank unleashed a wave of terror on the city. He sent South Side gang members to the polling booths with submachine guns and sawed-off shotguns to make sure that local residents "voted right." Uncooperative voters were assaulted and blocked from voting. Frank led an attack on an opponent's campaign headquarters, ransacking his office and assaulting several campaign workers. One campaign worker was shot in both legs and detained with eight other campaign workers, to be released when Election Day was over.

As the Election Day turmoil progressed, outraged Cicero citizens petitioned Cook County Judge Edmund J. Jareki for help. The Chicago Police Department (CPD) sent 70 plainclothes officers to Cicero to maintain order at the polls and Jareki swore them in as deputy sheriffs. The CPD officers fought battles with the South Side Gang around Cicero all day. Around mid-day, approximately 30 officers arrived in nine cars outside a polling station near the Western Electric plant. Already at the station, Frank and Al Capone allegedly thought these officers in civilian clothing members of the rival North Side Mob attacking them. According to police, Frank pulled out a handgun and fired at the officers. However, some bystanders said that Frank never got the gun out of his back pocket. In either event, the officers opened fire, killing Frank with dozens of shots.[3] Al managed to escape unharmed.

Enraged at Frank's death, Al retaliated by murdering one official and kidnapping others, and by stealing ballot boxes from the polling stations. At the end of the day, the Capone candidate Klenha had won.

After Frank's death, the Chicago newspapers were full of articles either praising or condemning the CPD. A coroner's inquest later determined that Frank's killing was a justifiable shooting since Frank had been resisting arrest.

On April 4, 1924, Frank Capone received an extravagant funeral, with $20,000 worth of flowers placed around the silver-plated casket and over 150 cars in the motorcade. Ironically, Al purchased the flowers from a shop belonging to his North Side Gang rival, Dion O'Banion.

Frank was interred at Mount Olivet Catholic Cemetery in Chicago. The Chicago Tribune reported that the event was appropriate for, "....a fitting gentleman." Out of respect for his dead brother, Al Capone closed the gambling dens and speakeasies of Cicero for two hours during the funeral.

The late Mr. Castucci

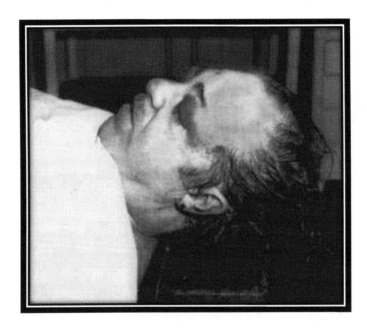

Richie Castucci was a Boston mob snitch, who owned the Ebb Tide lounge on Revere Beach, where the Teddy Deegan hit was plotted. In 1976 Castucci told the FBI where they could find fugitives Joe McDonald and James Simms. The FBI agents on the Winter Hill Gangs payroll turned that information over the gang who then lured Castucci to Somerville, where he was shot in the head by Johnny Martorano. His body was found in the trunk of his Cadillac in Revere

The late Mr. Chiesa

Italian prefect Carlo Alberto Dalla Chiesa, his wife Emanuela Setti Carraro and Policeman Domenico Russo were murdered by the mob on September 3rd 1982. Dalla Chiesa had been sent to Palermo to fight the Mafia. He lost.

The late Mr. Chinnici

On July 29th 1983, a bomb attack in the center of Palermo, Italy killed Judge Rocco Chinnici, two policemen as well as several innocent bystanders. Chinnici was also murdered for his war on the mafia.

The late Mr. Cinene

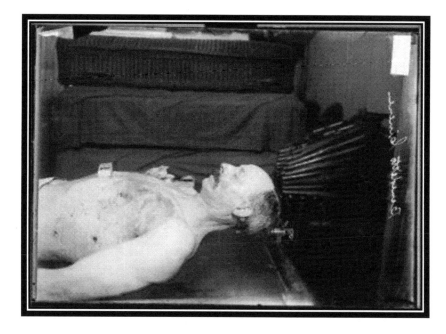

Gangster Bernedetto Cinene, murdered in Chicago on January 6, 1910

In January of 1910 the Chicago police raided six saloons believed to be run by members of the Black Hand, independent extortionist who preyed on the Italian-American community. The dragnet resulted in the arrest of 194 of Little Sicily's toughest criminals. Of the 194 persons arrested, 187 were fined and 7 discharged by the court. The sensational raid was the result of a need by the police to take action against Black Hand extortion and to avenge the death of Benedetto Cinene. Cinene had cooperated with the police in rescuing a 6-year-old boy who had been kidnapped in a recent Black Hand extortion case. Chicago authorities had hoped that the Little Sicily raid would lead them to information about the death of

Cinene and that the show of force might lead others to provide information to the police. It didn't. No one talked. The murder of Bernedetto Cinene went unsolved.

The late Mr. Coll

Vincent "Mad Dog" Coll (born Uinseann Ó Colla,) was a mob hitman in 1920s New York City. .After being expelled from multiple Catholic reform schools, he dropped out of school and joined The Gophers street gang where he became a protege of mobster Dutch Schultz.

Coll (right) and his wife (left)

Coll went to court to fight charges on the Vengalli killing. He retained famed defense lawyer Samuel Leibowitz. Leibowitz destroyed the credibility of the prosecution's main witness, George Brecht, a man who made a covert living as a witness at trials. In December 1931, Coll was acquitted.

In September 1931, between the killing of young Vengalli and his acquittal for that death, Coll was hired by Salvatore Maranzano, who had recently crowned himself the Mafia boss of all bosses in New York City, to murder his right-hand man, Charles "Lucky" Luciano. Luciano had previously helped Maranzano win the infamous Castellammarese War in New York and gain control of the New York Mafia. However, Maranzano suspected Luciano of wanting to kill Maranzano and seize power for himself.

The phone booth after the murder

Coll agreed to murder Luciano for a $25,000 payment in advance and a $25,000 payment on completion of the job. On September 10, 1931, Maranzano invited Luciano to visit his office. The plan was that Coll would turn up and kill Luciano. However, Luciano had received a tip-off about this plan (although probably not the identity of the hitman), so he instead sent over a squad of his own hitmen who stabbed and shot Maranzano to death. Coll finally arrived to kill Luciano, only to find Maranzano dead and Luciano's hitmen fleeing the scene.

It was said that both Dutch Schultz and Owney Madden had put a $50,000 bounty on Vincent Coll's head. At one point, Schultz had actually walked into a Bronx police station and offered "a house in Westchester" to whoever killed Coll.

On February 1, 1932, four or five gunmen invaded a Bronx apartment which Coll was rumored to frequent and opened fire with pistols and submachine guns. Three people (Coll gangsters Patsy Del Greco, Fiorio Basile, and bystander Emily Torrizello) were killed. Three others were wounded. Mad Dog himself didn't show up until thirty minutes after the shooting.

A week after the Bronx shootings, at 12:30 a.m. on February 8, Mad Dog Coll was using a phone booth in the London Chemists drug store at Eighth Avenue and 23rd Street. He was reportedly talking to Owney Madden, demanding $50,000 from the gangster under the threat of kidnapping his brother-in-law. Madden kept Coll on the line while the call was traced. Three men soon arrived in a dark limousine. While one waited behind the wheel, two others stepped out. One of them waited outside while the other walked inside, told the cashier to "Keep cool, now", drew a Thompson submachine gun from under his overcoat and opened fire on Coll in the glass phone booth. A total of fifteen bullets were dug out of Vincent Coll's body at the morgue; even more may have passed clean through him. The killers were chased unsuccessfully up Eighth Avenue by a foot patrolman who had heard the gunshots and commandeered a passing taxi.

The late Mr. Colombo

Joe Colombo served in the US Coast Guard during World War 2 but was given a medical discharge due to his increasing mental instability. (For which he received a pension) He went to work on the docks in New York, collecting a check from the Pride Meat Co., which was owned by Paul Gambino, brother of Carlo Gambino. Eventually Colombo associated himself with the Profaci Crime Family and became a made member of the mob in the mid-1950s.

Joe Colombo (FBI)

Colombo went out of his way to project an image of a dark suited, calm, businessman, but he was noted and feared for his enormous flair up, hair trigger temper and an astounding ability to assume everything and anything negative was being said about him.

He was made a Capo in the very early 1960s and was suspected of leading the Profaci's murder squad that police believe killed at least 16 people, perhaps more. When Joseph Profaci died of cancer in 1962, his brother-in-law, Guiseppe Magliocco took over the family officially, but many assume the real power behind the organization was the ever ambitious Joe Bonanno.

Bonanno, who wanted to rule the Underworld, called on Colombo to murder Carlo Gambino, Thomas Lucchese, and Stefano Magaddino. Instead, Colombo took Bonanno's message to Carlo Gambino. In turn, Gambino called a meeting of the New York families in which Bonanno and Magliocco were to stand trial. Only Magliocco showed up at the meeting and was fined $50,000 and forced to retire. As for Colombo, Gambino exerted pressures and the young Colombo, only 40 at the time, was given control over the Profaci family.

Tommy Lucchese before the Kefauver committee

Colombo inherited a family, then called the Profaci Crime family, wracked by internal warfare, dissent and the leaning pressure of Boss Carlo Gambino. However, Colombo was a moderately good manager and under his direction the Profaci's became big earners. Colombo himself became remarkably rich.

In the spring of 1970, Colombo foolishly responded to increasing FBI scrutiny of Mafia activity overall by picketing FBI offices in New York City, on the ridiculous grounds that the Bureau was harassing Italian-Americans. The push behind his actions was the April 30, 1970, the FBI arrested his son, Joe Jr., charging him with illegally melting $500,000 worth of U.S. coins containing silver.

To add pressure to the Bureau, Colombo organized the Italian-American Civil Rights League and as a show of strength, on June 29, 1970, 50,000 people showed up in Columbus Circle in New York City for an Italian-American Unity Day rally, in part, organized by Colombo. Among the participants were five U.S. Representatives and several prominent entertainers. He followed the Columbus day rally with a benefit for the League, headlines by Frank Sinatra in November of 1970, held at Madison Square Garden.

Colombo began to worry the Mobs old guard when he sought out the spotlight, appearing on the nightly news to rave against the FBI. At one point he even appeared on a nation-wide talk show. By 1980, the organization had 150,000 members with 50 chapters nationwide, which raised more than a million dollars and, in March of 1971, Colombo was, predictably, pronounced "Man of the Year" by the organization .

Colombo planned to follow up on the League's early successes by planning a second Italian Unity Day rally in Columbus Circle to be held June 28, 1971. Prior to the rally, Colombo's position became more difficult with the release from prison of. Gallo had previously battled for control of the Profaci/Colombo organization during the "Gallo-Profaci War." Gallo used his time in prison to build alliances with other ethnic criminals (most particularly black criminals in Harlem and the Bedford-Stuyvesant section of Brooklyn), and was using these contacts to disrupt Colombo's activities in Brooklyn.

On the morning of the rally, Colombo was shot by Jerome Johnson, an African American with a long criminal record and more than probably working for Crazy Joe Gallo. Johnson got close to Colombo by disguising himself as a newspaper photographer.

As Colombo made his way to the stage to address the rally, Johnson came up behind and fired off several rounds, hitting Colombo three times in the neck and head, seriously wounding Colombo but not killing him. However, he never regained consciousness. He lingered on in a coma for nearly seven years and died at his New Jersey estate on May 22, 1978.

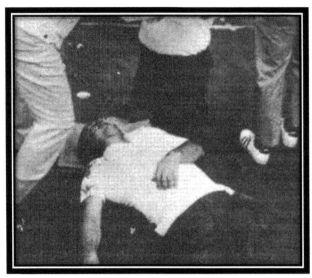

Colombo dying

After firing the shots, Johnson turned to run but was leaped on by Colombo's sons and body guards. There was a short struggle and shots were fired and Johnson was dead. Carlo Gambino also was considered a suspect, supposedly angered over Colombo's publicity and supported by the fact that Johnson was associated with the Gambino's, but its doubtful, Gambino was making money from Colombo's Anti-Italian-American League.

The late Mr. Colosimo

Giacomo Colosimo, AKA Big Jim Colosimo, was an Italian-American Mafia crime boss who built a criminal empire in Chicago based on prostitution, gambling, and racketeering.

When prohibition went into effect in 1920, his underboss, Johnny Torrio pushed for the gang to enter into bootlegging, but Colosimo refused. In May 1920, Colosimo went out of town to marry his second wife, Dale Winter (he had deserted his first wife).

After Colosimo returned to Chicago a week later, Torrio called him and let him know about a shipment arriving at his cafe. When Colosimo appeared at the cafe to wait for its delivery, he was shot and killed. The initial murder suspect was his new wife Dale, but no one was ever arrested for the murder.

It was widely believed that Torrio ordered Colosimo's killing so that the gang could enter the lucrative bootlegging business. Torrio reportedly brought in New York colleague, Frankie Yale, to murder Colosimo. Al Capone has also been suspected as Colosimo's assassin

The late Mr. Daugherty

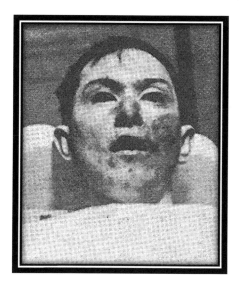

Chicago gunman for hire Red Daugherty in repose after the Capone mob caught up with him.

The Late Mr. Davis

Eddie Davis was a Chicago Knock around guy who sinned against the mob one to many times before Capone's men caught up with him in a speakeasy and killed him,

Death's Corner

Milton and Oaks Streets in Chicago. Between 1919 and 1930 over 15 gangsters were killed here

The late Mr. DeBatte

Mike DeBatte's body

Michael "The Bat" DeBatte was killed on orders of the Gambino family gangster Salvatore "Sammy the Bull" Gravano on November 2, 1987. The gunners caught up with him in Tali's Bar in Brooklyn.

The late Mr. DeMeo

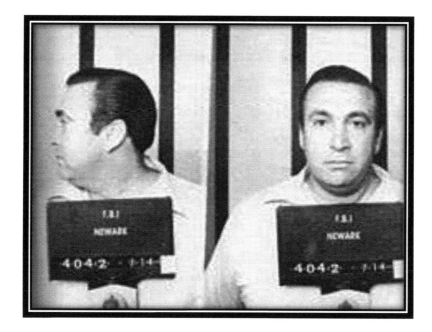

Roy Albert DeMeo was a soldier in the Gambino crime family. He is infamous for heading the "DeMeo crew", a gang suspected by the FBI of murdering at least 70 people between 1973 and 1983. The vast majority were disposed of so thoroughly that they were never found. The crew also gained notoriety due to their use of dismemberment as a method of disposing of their victims.

With the exception of killings intended to send a message to any who would hinder their criminal activities, or murders that presented no other alternative, a set method of execution was established by DeMeo and crew to ensure that victims would be dispatched quickly and then made to disappear. The method of execution was dubbed the "Gemini Method", named after the Gemini Lounge, the primary hangout of the DeMeo crew as well as the site where most of the crew's victims were killed.

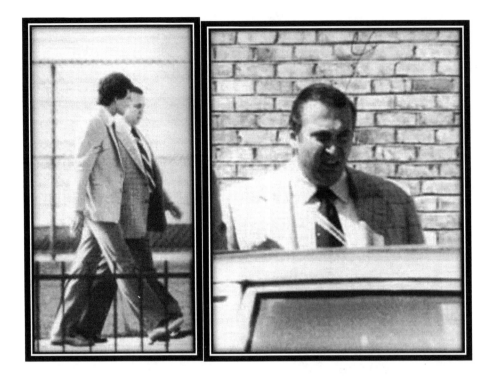

The exact process of the Gemini Method, revealed by multiple crew members and associates who became government witness in the early 1980s, was as follows: typically, the victim would be lured through the side door of the Lounge, and into the apartment that made up the back portion of the building. At this point, a crew member (almost always DeMeo according to crew member turned government witness Frederick DiNome) would approach with a silenced pistol in one hand and a towel in the other, shooting the victim in the head then wrapping the towel around the victim's head wound like a turban in order to staunch the blood flow.

Immediately after, another member of the crew (originally Chris Rosenberg up until his 1979 murder, according to government witness testimony) would stab the victim in the heart in order to prevent any more blood from pumping out of the gunshot wound. By then the victim would be dead, at which point the body would be stripped of its clothing and dragged into the bathroom where it was left while the remaining blood drained out and/or congealed within the body. This was to eliminate the messiness of the next step, when crew members would place the body onto plastic tarps laid out in the main room and proceed to dismember it, cutting off the arms, legs and head.

The body parts would then be put into bags, placed in cardboard boxes and sent off to the Fountain Avenue Dump in Brooklyn, where so many tons of garbage were dropped each day that it was a near impossibility for the bodies to ever be discovered. During the initial stages of an early 1980s Federal/State task force targeting the DeMeo crew, a plan by authorities to excavate sections of the dump in order to locate remains of victims was aborted when it was deemed too costly and likely to fail at locating any meaningful evidence.

Some victims would be killed in other ways for varying reasons. At times, suspected informants or those who committed an act of disrespect against a member of the crew or their superiors had their bodies left in the streets of New York to serve as a message and warning. As well, there were occasions where it would not be possible to lure the intended victim into the Gemini Lounge, in which case other locations would have to be used. A yacht owned by one of DeMeo's men was used on at least one occasion to dispose of bodies as well.

Dominick Montiglio, who visited DeMeo frequently to pick up payments for Anthony Gaggi, said in an interview that if the crew did not kill at least three people a week, they would be depressed.

By 1982, the FBI was investigating the enormous number of missing and murdered persons who were linked to DeMeo or who had last been seen entering the Gemini Lounge. It is around this time that an FBI bug in the home of Gambino family soldier Angelo Ruggiero picked up a conversation between Angelo and Gene Gotti, a brother of John Gotti.

In the conversation, it is discussed that Paul Castellano had put out a hit on DeMeo, but was having difficulty finding someone willing to do the job. Gene Gotti mentions that his brother John was wary of taking the contract, as DeMeo had an "army of killers" around him. It is also mentioned in this same secretly recorded conversation that, at that time, John had killed fewer than 10 people, while DeMeo had killed at least 38. According to mob turncoat Sammy Gravano, eventually the contract was given to Frank DeCicco, but Frank and his crew couldn't get to DeMeo either. DeCicco allegedly handed the job to DeMeo's own men.

Albert DeMeo wrote that in his final days, DeMeo was paranoid and knew that he would be killed soon. DeMeo considered faking his own death and leaving the country. However, instead he left the house one day and never returned. Albert DeMeo later found DeMeo's personal belongings such as his watch, wallet, and ring in his study room, and also a religious pamphlet indicating that DeMeo had gone to confession before his death.

According to the book Murder Machine, in his final days DeMeo was seen wearing a leather jacket, with a shotgun concealed underneath. On January 10, 1983, DeMeo went to crew member Patrick Testa's bodyshop for a meeting with his men. A few days later, on January 18, he was found murdered in his abandoned car's trunk. He had been shot multiple times in the head and had a bullet wound in his hand, assumed by law enforcement as being from throwing his hand up to his face in a self-defense reflex when the shots were fired at him.

The late Mr. Dickman

Billy Dickman was a Chicago hood who changed sides one to many times.

The late Mr. Dillenger

J. Edgar Hoover created a special task force headquartered in Chicago to locate bank robber and cop killer John Dillinger. Then, on July 21, 1933, a madam from a brothel in Gary, Indiana, Ana Cumpănaş, also known as Anna Sage, contacted the police. She was a Romanian immigrant threatened with deportation for "low moral character," and offered the federal agency information on Dillinger in exchange for their help in preventing her deportation. The agency agreed to her terms. Cumpănaş told them that Dillinger was spending his time with another prostitute, Polly Hamilton, and that she and the couple would be going to see a movie together on the following day. She agreed to wear an orange dress, which appeared red in the lights of the theater, so that police could easily identify her.

She was unsure which of two theaters they would be attending, but told the agency their names: the Biograph and the Marbro.

A team of federal agents and officers from police forces outside Chicago was formed. Chicago police officers were excluded because it was felt that the Chicago police had been compromised and could not be trusted. Not chancing another embarrassing escape, the police were split into two teams.

On July 22, one team was sent to the Marbro Theater on the city's west side, while another team surrounded the Biograph Theater at 2433 N. Lincoln Avenue on the north side. During the stakeout, the Biograph's manager thought the agents were criminals setting up a robbery. He called the Chicago police who dutifully responded and had to be waved off by the federal agents, who told them that they were on a stakeout for an important target

Dillinger attended the film Manhattan Melodrama at the Biograph Theater in Chicago's Lincoln Park neighborhood. Dillinger was with Polly Hamilton, and Ana Cumpănaș. Once they determined that Dillinger was in the theater, the lead agent (Samuel P. Cowley) contacted J. Edgar Hoover for instructions, who recommended that they wait outside rather than risk a gun battle in a crowded theater.

He also told the agents not to put themselves in harm's way, and that any man could open fire on Dillinger at the first sign of resistance. When the movie let out, Special Agent Melvin Purvis stood by the front door and signaled Dillinger's exit by lighting a cigar. Both he and the agents reported that Dillinger turned his head and looked directly at the agent as he walked by, glanced across the street, then moved ahead of his female companions, reached into his pocket but failed to extract his gun, and ran into a nearby alley.

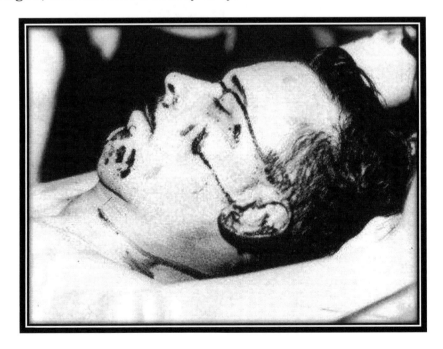

Agents Cowley, Purvis and Herman "Ed" Hollis opened fire, firing five shots. Dillinger was hit from behind and he fell face first to the ground. Two female bystanders were slightly wounded in the legs and buttocks by flying bullet and brick fragments. Dillinger was struck three times, twice in the chest, one actually nicking his heart, and the fatal shot, which entered the back of his neck and exited just under his right eye. Although three agents shot Dillinger, Charles Winstead was believed to be the man who fired the fatal shot, the one which went through Dillinger's head. An ambulance was summoned, though it was clear that Dillinger had quickly died from his gunshot wounds. At 10:50 p.m. on July 22, 1934, John Dillinger was pronounced dead at Alexian Brothers HospitalAccording to the investigators, Dillinger died without saying a wordThere were also reports of people dipping their handkerchiefs and skirts into the pools of blood that had formed as Dillinger lay in the alley in order to secure keepsakes of the entire affair. Dillinger's body was displayed to the public at the Cook County morgue after his death.

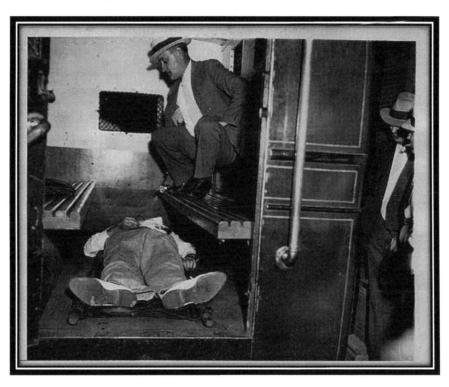

The Late Mr. Drucci

Vincent "The Schemer" Drucci, who may have been born under the name DiAmbrosio, served two years in the navy during World War I and receiving an honorable discharge. Coming home from war, he joined with other North Side gang then under Dion O'Bannon's control. After O'Bannion was murdered on Nov. 10, Drucci fell into a leadership position. One of his first acts was to order the drive by shooting of Capone's car on January 12, 1925. The attack was so vicious that Capone ordered a $30,000 bulletproof Cadillac as protection. A few days later, Weiss, Drucci and Moran shot and seriously wounded Johnny Torrio as he arrived home from an afternoon of shopping with his wife. Between May and November of 1925, Drucci was a suspect in three murders including Angelo Genna, shot gunned to death, Tony Genna, the third Genna bother to die within

44 days and the November 13 murders of gunmen "Samoots" Amatuna in a barbershop.

In at least one incident during that time, Drucci was drawn into a battle with Genna gunmen Scalise and Anselmi, who riddled Drucci's Getaway car slightly wounding Drucci.

On August 10, 1926 Drucci and Hymie Weiss walked towards Chicago's Standard Oil Building for a scheduled meeting with Morris Eller, a sanitary district trustee and the political boss of the 20th Ward. As Drucci and Weiss began to cross at Michigan and Ninth Streets, a car with three gunmen pulled up and began shooting at the two.

The Northsiders returned fire and in all, 30 shots were fired, only one bullet finding a target, a bystander. Weiss managed to escape before police arrived. Drucci leaped onto the running board of a passing car shouting at the driver "Take me away, and make it snappy," but police surrounded the car and arrested Drucci.

The North Siders retaliated with a spectacular drive by shooting
At the Hawthorne Inn in Cicero on the afternoon of September 20.

Hymie Weiss, leading a parade of at least ten cars, sprayed the place with over a thousand bullets, hoping to kill Capone. Remarkably, they missed.
Capone struck back. On October 11, ambushing and killing O'Bannion thug Hymie Weiss in front of the Holy Name Cathedral.
During the shooting ambush, one innocent citizen was killed and another three were wounded.

Detective Healy (right) turns over his weapon

The public was outraged by the murders and the public shooting
And was calling for a crackdown on the hoods. Capone called for a citywide peace conference at the Hotel Sherman where a five-point plan was drawn up and agreed to by the various gangs operating in the city. It worked, or at least it did for 70 days passed.

With peace filling the underworld, the hoodlums centered their attention on the upcoming mayoral election pitting incumbent mayor William E. Dever against former Mayor William Hale "Big Bill" Thompson.

On election day, Capone army of thugs were chased off of the streets in an effort to prevent the violence that marred previous election days. known hoods were picked up on sight by roving bands of Chicago police and the Illinois National Guard was on standby.

One election day eve, Drucci and several of his thugs kidnapping Alderman Dorsey Crowe, a Dever supporter. The night before, they had knocked out a watchman and ransacked Crowe's office.

On Monday, a squad of policemen spotted Drucci, Henry Finkelstein and Albert Single on the streets. The cops searched the three men and found a 45 automatic pistol on Drucci and arrested him and held the other two for questioning. Four policemen, including Patrolman Dan Healy and a lieutenant, were assigned to take the trio to the Criminal Courts Building where Green was waiting.
As they got into the squad cars, Healy and Drucci got into an argument because Drucci objected to Healy grabbing his arm. Drucci called Healy a name and Healy punched struck Drucci in the back of his head, pulled his service revolver and said, "Call me that again and I'll let you have it."

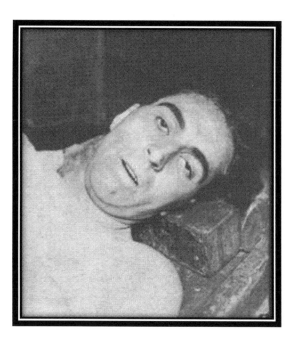

Drucci dead

According to Healy's statement Drucci continued to threaten him saying, "I'll get you, I'll wait on your doorstep for you." When told to shut up, Drucci responded, "Go on you kid copper, I'll fix you for this. Take your gun off and I'll kick hell out of you." And then claimed that

Drucci pinched him in the face and shouted, "I'll take you and your tool (gun)." And grabbed for the patrolman's pistol. Healy pulled his revolver and fired four times hitting Drucci with three shots.

Henry Finkelstein, one of Drucci's men said that Healy struck Drucci first. A scuffle began in the car and the driver pulled to a stop. One police officer exited the car, followed by Healy who abruptly stopped, turned on the running board and shot Drucci who was sitting with his hands on his lap. One way or the other, Drucci was shot in the left arm, right leg, and abdomen. He died on route to the hospital.

Drucci's attorney rushed to see Chief of Detectives William Shoemaker, demanding that Healy be arrested for murder. The chief replied "Arrest him? Hell We're thinking about giving medal was being g him a medal."
On April 7, Drucci's $10,000, surrounded by $30,000 in flowers, flag draped, aluminum and silver casket lay in the Sbarbaro funeral home, the place for Chicago's hoods to be waked.

The following day a crowd estimated at 1,000 followed the hearse, draped in an American flag to Mount Carmel Cemetery. There was a 21-gun salute by the honor guard, a bugler played taps and it was over. Drucci's wife was left with $40,000 in the estate. A substantial fortune for the time.

The (almost) late Mr. Eto

He was, in a mob filled with colorful and interesting gangsters, a very colorful and interesting gambler who ran a $200,000 a week bolita empire. In the papers he was called "Tokyo Joe" but in the mob he was Joe the Jap and the Yellow Italian. He was actually Korean-American. Eto learned gambling in the service while riding a troop train to Alaska during World War II. After returning to Chicago, he took up with the mob and handled not only their games and books, but also paid bribes to police, FBI Special agent Jack O'Rourke said. Since the 1950s, Eto controlled the bolita, an illegal lottery, in Chicago that made him a Multi- millionaire by the mid-1960s. "He was a trusted moneymaker, he'd been around for a long time and actually had kind of a reputation as a violent sort of person," said Elaine smith, former FBI agent. "Imagine what it would be like on a day-to-day basis and always show respect and always do what they said to do, unquestioning, with people that are dumb, immoral, selfish, corrupt individuals"

The Outfit had wrongly assumed that Eto had become an informant. In 1983, Eto was indicted and convicted of illegal gambling. While still awaiting a sentence, a maximum of 10 years, Joey Aiuppa thought that Eto couldn't or wouldn't do his time without cutting a deal and ordered him killed. After he was convicted and released on bail, Eto needed cash, that he could account for, and decided to sell the Marilou's restaurant, something that Auippa saw as another sign that Eto was entering the witness protection program.

Auippa feigned an interest in buying the restaurant and arranged to have his lieutenant, Joseph DiVarco to have Eto meet with Jasper Campise and John Gattuso, a Cook County deputy sheriff, in Maeilou's parking lot where he would be taken to Auippa. When Eto got here he was told that Auippa was called away and that they would have to meet again on the morning of Feburary 10, 1983. That day, DiVarco and Joe Arnold told Eto to meet Campise and Gattuso that evening and the three would talk at a West Side restaurant with North Side gambling boss Vincent Solano. After pulling into the Montclare Theater, 7129 W. Grand Avenue and shutting off the engine, Gattuso pulled out a .22 caliber pistol and shot Eto in the head three times. Eto wasn't badly hurt but had the good sense to slump down and play dead. The gun powder was old and the bullets, although fired, bounced off of Eto's head. Some investigators said the .22-caliber pistol used in the shooting might have had a defective silencer that greatly reduced the speed of the bullets.

Gattuso and Campise, then left him for dead. Eto didn't die, and after awaking from unconsciousness, dragged himself to a nearby pharmacy, where he called 911. That night, Eto started talking to the FBI. "He really had nowhere else to go," FBI agent O'Rourke said. During his cooperation, Eto admitted to a role in four murders. "He didn't participate in these murders, he set the people up," an FBI agent said The FBI learned that soon after the shooting, the mob planned to murder Gattuso and Campise and tried to persuade the men to cooperate with the government, but they refused. Instead, after they were bailed out of jail, driven to a parking lot of a Naperville Illinois condominium, stabbed, strangled and shot to death. Their bodies were then stuffed into the trunk of Campise's car and found four months later on July 14, 1983. Every major organ in their bodies had been slashed.

While testifying in 1985 President's Commission on Organized Crime, he spoke in hushed tones and whispers while wearing a hood. Eto testified that between 1980 and 1982 he paid cash bribes totaling $900 to State Representative James DeLeo, the first state legislator implicated in the Operation Greylord investigation of judicial corruption, a Democrat from Chicago to fix parking tickets at Traffic Court in Chicago "I'd walk away from Mr. DeLeo (in his Traffic Court office) and count it," Eto testified. "I walked back to Mr. DeLeo, folded it in my hand and shook his hand."

He said that he paid DeLeo about $150 "once or twice" a year between 1980 and 1982 to take care of parking tickets Eto accumulated when he lived at 21 E. Chestnut Street, a highly congested neighborhood. DeLeo, whose salary was $21,000 a year, owned a series of Corvettes, Cadillac's, a Jaguar and a Mercedes-Benz between 1978 and 1982.

In 1991, Eto testified in the trial of Ernest Rocco Infelice and Louis Marino that he paid protection money to Infelice and Marino, totaling about $50,000. "Five thousand a month." He said "Usually (paid) in the first week of the month. In person. Cash. One-hundred-dollar bills. Vince (Solano) asked me if I could pay $5,000 a month. I said, `Yes,' and he told me to give the money to Rocky (Infelice). Louie Marino would call me and set a date and time" at a West Side restaurant. "Usually, Rocky and Louie would come together, and I would pass the money under the table."

 He added that he considered Infelice and Marino to be his friends in the mob and that the money he paid was a blanket payment that allowed him to run a variety of gambling businesses, from bets on ethnic Chinese and Puerto Rican games to American-style card games, horse races and sports events. He said that in the early 1980s, when police raids in Chicago were making his life miserable, cutting his ability to make money and pay the mob, too, Infelice told him "Go to Lake County," because Eto said "Anywhere in Lake County, it belonged to them (the street crew)." But Eto stayed out of the county because it was too far for his Hispanic and Asian clientele to travel. In the 1970s, Eto wanted to open a strip club in suburban Lyons but was turned down by boss Joey Aiuppa. Because said Eto "Aiuppa reportedly controls Lyons' "sin strip." And didn't want any competition. "I was turned down."

He said Infelice told him "Don't feel bad that you got turned down. That is `sacred territory'," Eto, did however, own a fine dining restaurant in Lyons' called Marilou's. Eto's bleak testimony changed when the prosecutor asked him to look around the courtroom and point out the men he had been talking about. Infelice stood up, smiled at Eto and waved in his direction. So did Marino. "He (Infelice) is the man waving at me," Eto said, giggling and smiling back. He repeated himself when Marino stood up and waved.

77

Although law enforcement blamed the attempted murder of Joey Auippa, who certainly had to give his okay on the murder, Eto told the President's Commission on Organized Crime that Vincent Solano, a North Side crime syndicate rackets boss as well as president of Local 1 of the mob-linked Laborers' Union., ordered him killed and said that Solano was the mob's "ultimate source of power," Eto said, "Being able to corrupt and bribe city officials, politicians and policemen and instill fear in the general public by threats, intimidation and murder." Eto said that Solano ordered him killed for fear that he would spill mob secrets. Eto said he had been indicted by a federal grand jury on gambling charges and faced a prison term if convicted.

He said that he owned a night club called the Bourbon Street at 936 N. Rush Street which was enormously profitable, but he was forced to sign the club over to Solano's son. Though promised "compensation" for giving up the business, he was never paid. He said that for his protection money, a secret code was used by the bribed vice-detectives to alert the outfit about pending gambling raids on Eto's places "I'm just the furnace man. I'll be there in a couple of hours or a couple of days," was the message sent to Eto when something big was scheduled to go down.

He also was given mob muscle when he needed it. Eto once testified that Johnny Monteleone and enforcer John Fecarotta, a business agent for Local 8 of the Laborer's AFL-CIO Industrial Workers Union, supplied the muscle that kept the deadbeats in line. A customer who routinely disrupted the monte game was taken by car to a secret location where he was punished. While en route to the destination, the heel of Monteleone's shoe on the gambler's back kept him in place. Wielding a two-by-four, Fecarotta beat the man senseless. He lived on his last days in Georgia as Joe Tanaka, a restaurateur from Iowa, the father of six children.

The late Mr. Falcone

On May 23th 1992, the mafia killed Italian judge Giovanni Falcone, his wife Francesca Morvillo and the policemen Antonio Montinari, Rocco Di Cillo and Vito Schifani with a 500 pound bomb. Falcone had been both fearless and effective in his campaign to crush the mob in Italy.

The late Mr. Fay

Larry Fay's El Fay club.

Larry Fay was one of the early rumrunners of the Prohibition Era in New York City. He made a half a million dollars bringing whiskey into New York from Canada. With his profits he bought into a taxi cab company and later opened a nightclub, the El Fey, on West 47th Street in Manhattan in 1924, featuring Texas Guinan as the emcee and a floorshow produced by Nils Granlund.

 Fay, who had a record of forty-nine arrests but no felony convictions, was involved in several enterprises in the ensuing years, and was said to have amassed and lost a fortune. He was made a partner of the Casa Blanca Club, where he was shot four times after a 1932 New Year's Eve celebration by the club's doorman who had just learned his pay was being reduced by Fay to accommodate a new employee. He died the next day.

The late Mr. Ferlito

On June 16th 1982, a rival Mafia fraction in Italy killed boss Alfio Ferlito and murdered the four policemen who was escorting him to prison

The late Mr. Ferrigno

Stefano Ferrigno being carried to his grave

On November 4, 1930, a meeting of Boss Joe Masseria supporters was held in Ferrigno's Bronx apartment at 759 Pelham Parkway South. In attendance were believed to be a number of top Masseria and Mineo crime family members, including Mineo, Lucky Luciano, Vito Genovese, Masseria and Stefano Ferrigno. Observing the meeting from across a courtyard were Maranzano faction members Joe Profaci, Nick Capuzzi and Joe Valachi. According to Valachi, in the night of November 5, 1930, Steve Ferrigno and Al Mineo left the apartment and walked across the courtyard, and the Maranzano men mowed them down with gunfire from a high powered rifle.

Al Mineo, dead

The late Mr. Floyd

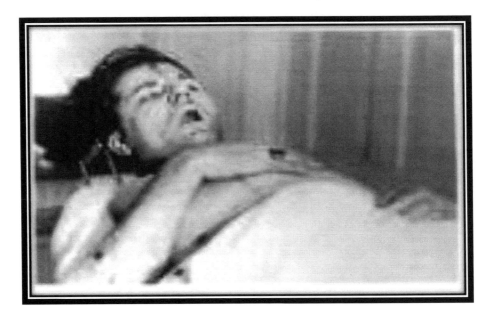

According to the FBI, four FBI agents, led by Agent Melvin Purvis, and four members of the East Liverpool Police Department, led by Chief Hugh McDermott, were searching the area south of Clarkson, Ohio, in two separate cars for bank robber Pretty Boy Floyd. They spotted a car move from behind a corn crib, and then move back. Floyd then emerged from the car and drew a .45 caliber pistol, and the FBI agents opened fire. Floyd reportedly said: "I'm done for. You've hit me twice."

  However, Chester Smith, the retired East Liverpool Police Captain and sharpshooter, described events differently in a 1979 interview for Time magazine. Smith, who was credited with shooting Floyd first, stated that he had deliberately wounded, but not killed, Floyd. He then added: "I knew Purvis couldn't hit him, so I dropped him with two shots from my .32 Winchester rifle." According to Smith's account, after being wounded, Floyd fell and did not regain his footing. Smith then disarmed Floyd. At that point, Purvis ran up and ordered: "Back away from that man. I want to talk to him." Purvis questioned Floyd briefly, and after receiving curses in reply ordered agent Herman "Ed" Hollis to "Fire into him." Hollis then shot Floyd at point-blank range with a submachine gun, killing him. The interviewer asked if there was a cover-up by the FBI, and Smith responded: "Sure was, because they didn't want it to get out that he'd been killed that way." This account is extremely controversial. If true, Purvis effectively executed Floyd without benefit of judge or jury.

Floyd's body was embalmed and briefly viewed at the Sturgis Funeral Home, in East Liverpool, Ohio before being sent on to Oklahoma. Floyd's body was placed on public display in Sallisaw, Oklahoma. His funeral was attended by between 20,000 and 40,000 people and remains the largest funeral in Oklahoma history. He was buried in Akins, Oklahoma.

The late Mr. Galante

Carmine Galente and bodyguard, dead

Carmine Galante C AKA Lilo, the Cigar was an ignorant and crass man, who stood just under five feet with a barrel frame, Galante was the son of a fisherman who immigrated from Castellammare del Golfo in Sicily to an East Harlem tenement where Galante was born and raised.

Galante in his later life and as a young hood in 1945 (NYPD photos)

His criminal career began about 1921, when, at the age of eleven, Galante started a teenage gang that practiced extortion on local shop keepers. Several years later, while still in teens, he became an enforcer for various bootleg gangs during prohibition. In 1930, Galante, with several others, were caught by New York police officer Joseph Meenahan while attempting to hijack a truck in the Williamsburg, a neighborhood in Brooklyn. A gun battle broke out and Galante shot the beat cop through the leg. He also fired off a fatal bullet that struck an innocent six-year-old girl who was standing along the sidewalk watching the mayhem. Although both survived Galante was sentenced to 12 1/2 years in prison and was released on parole in 1939. A year later, in 1940, he was working as a contract killer and all around thug for Boss Vito Genovese, then a powerful hood making his way up the Mafia ladder. Galante is widely suspected of carrying out the 1943 murder of Italian journalist Carlo Tresca as he walked along a New York street.

 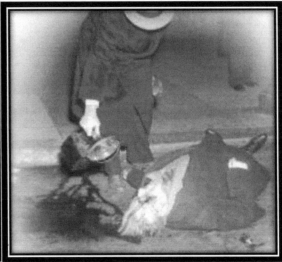

Carlo Tresca alive and dead

The order came from Genovese who wanted the reporter dead as a favor to Italian Dictator Benito Mussolini. During his getaway, a witness to the murder, wrote down Galante's license plate number as he sped away from the murder scene. Police determined that it was the same car Galante had driven earlier in the day, oddly enough, to visit his parole officer. He was arrested later that evening for a parole violation but released and was never held accountable for the brazen murder. It was at this point that Galante switched families and joined Joe Bonanno.

Shortly afterwards, Galante was promoted to driver for Joe Bonanno. He was made a Capo in the organization and then, in the very late 1960s, promoted to Underboss. However his rising career came to a temporary halt in 1962 when he was convicted on a series of narcotic charges and sentenced to twenty years in federal prison. Word in the Underworld was that Boss Frank Costello had engineered the arrest. While in prison, Galante was diagnosed with a "serious psychopathic personality disorder" although a Doctor in Sing Sing prison was more direct simply calling Galante "a psychopath"

Main Hall at Sing Sing Prison

He was released from prison in 1974. He was suspected of being directly involved in eight murders between 1975 and 1978, most of his victims being members of the rival Gambino crime family who were jousting with the Bonanno's and with Galante in particular, for control of the US heroin trade. Galante was arrested and jailed again in 1978 for a parole violation (Associating with known felons) he was released on appeal, his defense lawyer being the renowned Mob lawyer Roy Cohn.

One of Galante's more profitable but lesser known crimes was his preference to shake down, extort, money from other gangsters. It was a simple process. Galante would demand a cut of their operation or cash buy out to be left alone. If they refused to pay or took their complaint to their Capo, he would kill them. They all paid.

At about this time, in the early 1970s, Galante was instrumental in further developing the already prosperous the infamous French Connection, a drug trade network, which encompassed numerous countries and hundreds, if not thousands of criminals. The drug network imported Turkish Opium into France, then shipping it into French Canada and then bringing it into the United States.

When the money started to pour into his coffers and his own organization was springing up around him, Galante ordered the brass crypt doors of former gangster Frank Costello, blown off their hinges. (Although Costello had died in 1973 of natural causes) The message was that Galante was back and ready for war if they wanted it. No one challenged him.

From the very beginning of his release Galante had made it clear that he intended to take over the Bonanno family. At the time, the new boss was Philip "Rusty" Rastelli, although he was ruthless, was no match for Galante viciousness.

Rusty Rastelli

Rastelli was trying to rule the family from prison, but Galante, by sheer force, took over the Bonanno's. With Rastelli out of the way, Galante immersed himself in the drug trade. He was well on his way to controlling large parts of the international drug market which would make him extremely wealthy and powerful. With enough money and the guns money could buy, he could take over the entire American Mafia.

What bothered the bosses, aside from Galante greed, his willingness to murder without reason and his corner on the drug trade, was that he openly despised the Commission members who had forced Joe Bonanno to step down. More than once, he had threatened to murder Carlo Gambino. All of this made the bosses nervous. So they decided to kill Galante. Even Joe Bonanno agreed that Galante had to die.

July 12, 1979 was a warm, muggy summer day in Bushwick, Brooklyn. Gigante opted to have his lunch in the open air courtyard of Joe and Mary's Italian

American Restaurant, at 205 Knickerbocker Avenue. The restaurant owner was Galante's cousin,
Giuseppe Turano, also a Bonanno solider. Galante ate there often. It was a modest place with a full bar and small dining room with decent enough food. A large glass door opened to the patio where Galante could smoke his cigars in peace and discuss family business without interference. Galante arrived with his Capo Leonard "Nardo" Coppola and two body guards, Cesare Bonventre and Baldo Amato.

Baldo Amato

They were met by Angelo "Little Moe" Provenzano, a Bonanno solider. As they ate, Provenzano began to complain of stomach pains and Galante encourages him to go home and lay down until the pain passed.

As Provenzano left, one of the bodyguards excused himself to use the bathroom and the other guard left to make a phone call. About 2:55 . Galante finished his lunch and pulled out a fresh cigar and stuck it in his mouth. In his later years it was rare to see Gigante without an expensive cigar crushed between his teeth. But before he could get it lit, a group of masked men rushed into the courtyard from inside the restaurant, one of them carrying a shotgun. Outside the restaurant, Dominick "Big Trin" Trinchera was standing look out.

"Big Trin" Trinchera

With him was the operations driver, Santo Giodano. Joe Massino, Sonny Red Indelicato, J.B. Indelicato and Phil Lucky Giacone were also outside in a back-up car.

Joe Massino

Galante towards the end of his life

Inside, the gunmen rushed through the main dining hall. There is little doubt that Galante and Coppola saw them coming but didn't move, either out of fright or confusion.

The son of the restaurant owner was gunned done while reaching for a gun stashed in the back room. His father rushed to his aid and he was cut down. The shooters squared off and blasted Galante who was knocked out his chair, his cigar still protruding from his mouth. Two of the gunmen then turned on Lenny Copolla and fired on him, hitting him directly in the face, killing him.

The killers were Anthony Indelicato, Russell Mauro, Bruno Indelicato and Louie Giongetti. Each of the men was promoted after the killing. Anthony Indelicato, then 23 years old, was convicted of the murder, but not until 1986. He served 12 years in prison.

 Galante's body guards, Cesare Bonventre and Baldo Amato, also took part in the killing. Sources in the Underworld said that Gambino underboss Aniello Dellacroce set Galante up for the kill.

Cesare Bonventre

The late Mr. Gallo

New York boss Joe Profaci ruled with an iron fist for three decades and was widely hated by his men. In the old Sicilian style, he required every member of the family to pay him monthly dues of $25 in addition to the cut he took for simply being the boss. The extra $25 tax was supposed to cover of legal fees, bribes and support payments to a soldier's family if he was imprisoned, but few if any in the family actually reaped the benefits yet anyone who held out was killed. Although he ruled over Brooklyn, Profaci lived in a massive mansion on a 328-acre estate on Long Island, which held a hunting lodge and private airport.

In 1961, a group led by Joey Gallo rebelled against Profaci's rule (In part stirred behind the scenes by power mad Carlo Gambino) In early in 1962, Gambino suggested that Profaci retire. The Mafia's national Commission, however, gave him a vote of confidence that year. But Profaci died of cancer shortly after receiving the Commission's backing.

Upon his death, Joe Magliocco took the reins of the Profaci Family, and civil war with the Gallo group broke out and lasted until 1962.

Joey Gallo went to prison for a while, got out and decided to take over so the bosses decided he had to go. On his forty-third birthday, April 7, 1972, Gallo decided to dine at Umberto's Clam House in Manhattan's Little Italy. Joey Gallo and his bodyguard were relaxed and made the mistake of sitting with their backs to the door. A gunman came in and fired at Gallo with an automatic revolver. Gallo was hit, but managed to walk outside, where he collapsed and died.

The late Mr. Garofalo

Edward Garofalo

Eddie Garafalo wasn't a made guy in the Gambino family but he stiull had to pay them when he made a fast buck but he decided not to. So as soon as Garofalo finished a 90-day sentence for dumping of medical waste, Sammy the Bull Gravano's men tracked him down to 83d St. in Dyker Heights, Brooklyn and shot him dead.

The Bloody Genna's

The Bloody Genna's

Al Capone and Dion O'Bannon's deadliest competitors were the Genna Brothers. In May of 1923, Brother Angelo had met his fate a few days after his honeymoon, at the hands of O'Bannionite Bugs Moran. Driving down a central street, Genna came across Moran and several other O'Bannionites who were driving in the opposite direction.

Moran ordered the car turned around and chased Genna for a few miles, caught up to Genna's car and fired a volley of shotgun blasts into his head, killing him instantly. Three weeks later, Moran approached one of the Genna's bodyguards with an offer to set up two of Genna's most lethal gunmen, John Scalise and Albert Anselmi.

Ogden and Hudson where Angelo Genna was killed

In exchange for bribe, Moran wanted the bodyguard to lure the Italians to the corners of Sangamon and Congress Streets on June 13th at 9:00 A.M. The bodyguard agreed to the set up but informed Scalise and Anselmi anyway.
On the morning of the 9th, Bugs Moran and "Schemer" Drucci waited in their car for the Italians to arrive, when suddenly a black limousine swung by their car and filled it with shotgun pellets, wounding both of the O'Bannionites, who returned fire, but were too shot up to give chase.

Instead, they crawled out of the car, limped to a nearby hospital where they stayed for several weeks recuperating from their wounds. Meanwhile, the drive-by limousine, which contained Genna gunmen Mike Genna at the wheel and Scalise and Anselmi on guns in the back seat, speeded down the street and almost sideswiped an unmarked police car carrying Irish American police detective Michael Conway, Rookie William Sweeny, officer Charles Walsh and another officer, Harold Olson.

Tony Genna murder spot

Recognizing Mike Genna, the policemen gave chase through the city streets at 70 miles an hour, finally overtaking the gangsters' limousine after it smashed into a telephone pole. The three gangsters hopped out of the car, shotguns in hand. The squad car pulled up a few seconds later and detective Conway leaped out first and was cut down first. Next, the hoodlums killed Walsh and Olson, leaving only the rookie policeman, Sweeny, unwounded to shoot it out. Sweeny covered himself behind the squad car and fired several shots at the gangsters who fired back and then fled across an empty field. Sweeny gave chase.

Anselmi and Scalise disappeared into a nearby alley, leaving their boss Mike Genna alone to shoot it out with the detective Sweeny. Out of breath, Genna stopped and turned on the oncoming police and raised his shotgun and pulled the trigger only to find both barrels empty. Sweeny fired off a blast into Genna's leg and the bullet lodged in a main artery. By now the area was flooded with dozens of policemen who found Genna hiding in the basement of a house he had broken into to elude the manhunt.

He had lost too much blood, an ambulance was called, the dying Genna placed inside. As they sped to the hospital, a guard lowered his face close to the gangster and asked if he was comfortable. Genna kicked him in the face, "Take that you son of a bitch!" He died a few minutes later. Anselmi and Scalise were arrested a short time later, trying to escape on a railroad car.

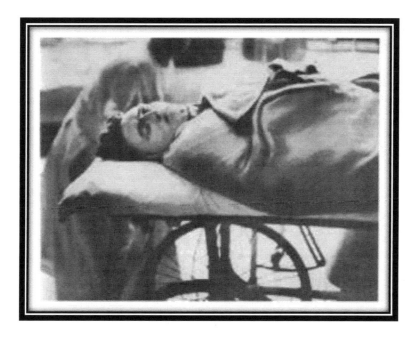

Tony Genna dying

A few weeks later, Tony Genna was gunned down in a grocery store in an almost exact duplication of the Dion O'Bannion murder. As Tony shook the hand of an associate, someone came up behind him and shot him through the head.

Cops examine the Genna arsnal

Tony and Mike Genna were buried together in Mount Carmel cemetery, Chicago's Boot Hill. When one policeman, sent to witness the burial noticed the Italians' gravesite was only a few feet from Dion O'Bannon's tomb, he said: "When judgment day comes and them three graves are opened, there'll be hell to pay in this cemetery."

The late Mr. Giaccone

Dr. Paolo Giaccone was murdered in Palermo on August 13, 1982, because he refused to create fake hospital files to save boss Filippo Marchese from jail

The late Mr. Giancana

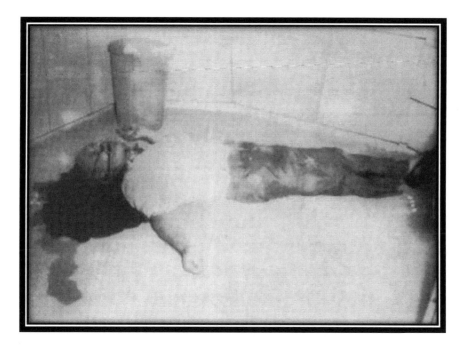

Chicago boss Sam Giancana was an example of a man who had worn out his welcome. Extradited from Mexico to the US to face charges and answer questions about the Kennedy-Cuba issues, Sam was in hot water with Chicago boss Tony Accardo. Giancana had been running gambling operations there without sending money back to the Accardo operation and once you're in, the only way out is feet first. On July 19, 1975 Giancana somebody shot a "happy face" around the Giancana's mouth, killing him.

The late Mr. Green

Danny Green

Daniel "Danny" J. Patrick Greene was an associate of Cleveland mobster John Nardi during the gang war for the city's criminal operations during the 1970s.

On October 6, 1977, Greene went to a dental appointment at the Brainard Place office building in Lyndhurst, Ohio. Members of the Mafia had tapped his phone and were aware of the visit. After Greene's dental visit, he left the office building and approached his car. The automobile parked next to his exploded, killing Greene instantly

The late Mr. Gioe

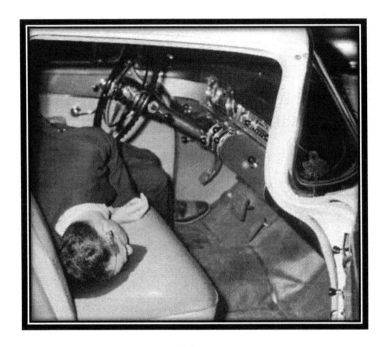

Gioe

On August 18, 1954, Charles Gioe AKA Cherry Nose, was shot to death by killers working for Chicago Capo Joey Glimco after Gioe got between Glimco AKA Little Ceaser, in a dispute Glimco was having with a contractor building a Howard Johnson's restaurant.

The late Mr. Greenberg

The Hickory Pit, the South Side restaurant where 'Louie Greenberg was killed

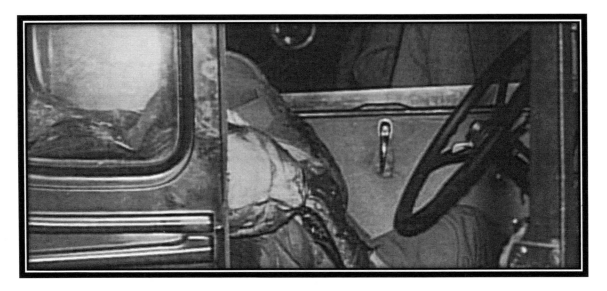

Greenberg, dead

Louis Greenberg, 64, was an ego centric cheap skate and informer, who cheated Frank Nitti's family out of enormous sums of cash entrusted to him by Nitti before his suicide. Frank Nitti's window, Annette, told Boss Paul Ricca that Frank Nitti had been turning over cash and securities to Greenberg to hold for safe keeping and by the time Nitti killed himself Greenberg was said to be holding at least $2 million of his cash. Yet, of that amount Greenberg paid out only $164,500 into the trust of Nitti's ten-year-old adopted son Joseph. And, said Mrs. Nitti said that Greenberg talked her into signing a release stating that the legal claims to the boy's trust had been satisfied. Paul Ricca sent Tony Accardo to talk over the problem with Greenberg who agreed to pay the family the money he owed them. However, he only paid what he termed "interest on capital." That was enough. On December 8, 1955, he was shot and stabbed to death as he and his second wife Pearl left the Glass Dome, a hickory barbecue place where they often dined.

The Late Miss Hill.

After her boyfriend Bugsy Siegel was murdered by the mob, Virginia Hill continued working for the Chicago outfit as a courier for several more years before they replaced her in 1950. She married a guy who wasn't involved with the outfit and had a child, but that ended in divorce. Joey Epp never fell out of love with her, and he kept her on the books for as long as they bosses would let him, but eventually even that stopped. When it did, it was widely rumored in gangland that Virginia, desperate for cash, started to extort money out of Joe Adonis and other mob guys for whom she had carried narcotics over the years. On March 24, 1966, near a brook in Koppl Austria, a small town near Salzburg, two hikers found Virginia Hill's dead body. Austrian officials, not understanding who Hill had been, ruled her unusual death a suicide by poison.

The late Mr. Hitchcock

Burham Illinois bootlegger Frank Hitchcock decided to horn in on beer routes that belonged to the Burnham's town mayor, Johnny Patton AKA The boy mayor and a Capone loyalist. Hitchcock was called to Patton's office, shot and killed and dumped into the corn field in the back yard.

The late Mr. Howard.

Joe Howard

Joseph W. Howard, age 28, AKA Ragtime Joe as he liked to be called, was a small time hood who lived above his mother's fruit store in Chicago. One night Howard was in a gambling den owned and operated by Capone men Jack Guzick and Denny Cooney. Howard leaned on Guzik for a $1,500 loan which Guzik refused. He may or may not have slapped Guzik. On May 8th, 1924, Howard went to Hymie Jacobs' saloon for a drink. At around 6:30, Al Capone walked in and Howard said to him "Hello Al" but Capone grabbed Howard by the collar and fired six bullets into his face and right shoulder.

The late Mr. Inzerillo

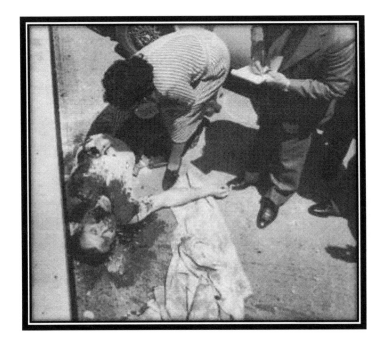

Salvatore Inzerillo was the boss of Passo di Rigano family in Corleone Italy until he was killed on May 11th 1981. The Mafia usurpers then killed several of his relatives, including his fifteen year old son Giuseppe.

The late Mr. Genova

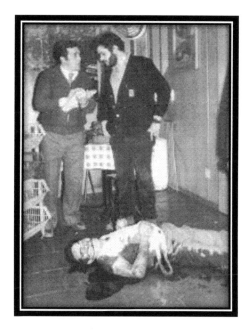

Giuseppe Genova was the son-in-law of Sicilian Mafia boss Tommaso Buscetta. Genova was sitting in a pizzeria on December 26, 1982 when he was gunned down along with his nephews Orazio and Antonio D'Amico.

The late Mr. Jaworski

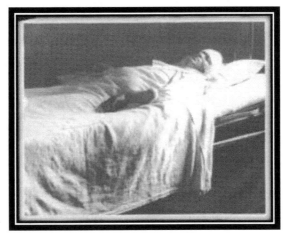

Paul Jaworski in a Cleveland Hospital on September 24, 1928 after an underworld misunderstanding. Jaworski was the leader of the "Flatheads" gang, who committed the first-ever armored car robbery, on March 11, 1927. They placed a landmine under the roadbed, and made off with money. Jaworski was eventually sentenced to death in Pennsylvania . He was executed on January 21, 1929, by electric chair for a separate payroll robbery which resulted in a murder.

The late Mr. Lanzetti

Police recover the body of gangster Willie Lanzetti from underbrush in Wynnewood, Pennsylvania. 1939

The late Mr. Lima

Salvo Lima, a Sicilian political leader was murder by the Mafia on March 12, 1992 in retaliation for the stiff sentences handed down by the courts on Mafia members.

The Late Jake Lingle

Chicago hustler Jake Lingle came from a moderately successful Irish working class family in the valley, an Irish slum near the Loop. In a single generation, the valley produced some of Chicago's finest and most capable leaders and some of its most notorious criminals. Lingle, smart, quick and affable, knew them all

Although Lingle managed to graduate from the Calhoun elementary school he otherwise ill prepared to work as for the Chicago Tribune newspaper as a reporter for $65 a week, a respectable salary in 1933. His superiors soon learned that Lingle was in over his head as a reporter, he couldn't write and he had no desire for accuracy or a follow through. He was reduced to the status of a "Legman"-- a street man who gathered the news and called it in to the city editor's room, where the stories were written by professional news writers.

Despite his humble background and limited intellectual abilities and a small income Lingle was chauffeured around town in a limo and was known to drop

$1000 a day on the horse races and he boasted, often and loudly, about the diamond studded belt he wore that had been given to him by Al Capone.

What gave his wealth was the fact that Lingle was a liaison between the Capone organization and police commissioner, Irish -American William P. Russell. Lingle and Russell had known each other since their childhood days in the Valley. Later, after Lingle was dead and the facts of their relationship came to light, Russell resigned his position.

Through Lingle's connection with the commissioner and the higher ups in the police department, he was able to pass on confidential police information to the Capone's, and others willing to pay, about what speakeasies were to be raided, what brothels were marked to be shut down and so forth. Lingle also spied on Bugs Moran and his North Siders for Capone.

No definite link was ever made between Lingle and Russell as far as kick back payments were concerned, but it is highly unlikely that a small timer like Lingle would have access to the type of high level intelligence information he had, with out Russell's consent.

Lingle was also a degenerate gambler who owed Capone $100,000 in gambling debts. He decided to pay it off by first trying to extort north side gangster Bugs Moran and later Capone. Lingle offer was if the gangsters would forgive his debts he would use influence to barter gambling and liqueur licenses, essential to both hoodlums' operations, for them. He also wanted a cut from the licenses he delivered.

It was a nervy thing to do but that was Lingle. One of the hundreds of rumors going around the city at that time was that Lingle had been given $50,000 to keep a Moran-Capone owned racetrack open but that he had pocketed the money anyway and as a result the track was closed.   Another story involved the Sheridan Club, a bar owned and operated by Moran gangster Hymie Weiss which had been closed for eighteen months after the St. Valentine's Day murders. Moran tried to muster help to reopen the track with no luck until a hustler named Julian "Potatoes" Kaufman approached Lingle on Moran's behalf and asked him to use his contacts to get the Moran's track reopened. Lingle said he would help, but for 50% of the profits. Moran refused and the club remained closed.

Moran turned to John "Boss" McLaughlin for advice. McLaughlin, also a product of the valley and a criminal mastermind who occasionally worked with the Touhy organization on burglaries, hated Lingle and had once threatened to kill the newsman when he refused to intercede in obtaining police and Capone's permission to open a gambling house. It was McLaughlin's advice that Moran go to the State's Attorney's office with the information he had on Lingle but Moran decided against it. He decided it was cleaner to simply murder the reporter.

At the same time, Capone had reached the same conclusion. Supposedly Lingle had gone to Capone and promised that for a set price he would see to it that no more of Capone's speakeasies were shut down. When Capone refused, Lingle threatened to have one of Capone's speakeasies shut down every day until Lingle got his price.

So Lingle was a dead man. On the day they killed Lingle, his killers, dressed as Roman Catholic priests followed Lingle across town. As Lingle entered a subway tunnel, one of the two killers ran up from behind Lingle and fired a round off into the reporter's head just as Lingle walked into an underground pass at Randolf and Michigan, his face buried in the daily racing form. It was at rush hour and a dozen citizens were in or near the tunnel when Lingle was gunned down. Lingle had $1400 in his pocket when he was killed. Russel resigned shortly afterwards.

The Lingle murder investigation dogged Chicago's gangland throughout the summer and fall. Citizens demanded action. Unaware that Lingle was mixed up with criminals, the Chicago newspapers promise a $55,000 reward for information on the murderer.

The murder became worldwide news and the police demanded that Capone turn over the men who had killed Lingle but Capone refused saying instead that he would have his execution squad take out the killer, which would bring an end to the matter. In retaliation, the Chicago police cracked down on the underworld and for a while, a very brief while, the hoods found it difficult to operate in Chicago.

Eventually, a professional small time criminal named Leo Brothers, a one time member of the Irish gang Egan's Rats in St. Louis, was arrested in connection with the crime. He was already wanted in St. Louis in questioning for another murder.

His trial began March 16, 1931, and ended on April 2, 1931, when he was convicted of murder and sentenced to eight years. Brothers was sentenced to 14 years in prison even though it was widely assumed Brothers was a fall guy for the killing. He was paroled eight years later. He returned to St. Louis and went to work for the mob as a union font man. He died of a heart attack in 1950.

The Late Patsy Lolordo

Pasqualino "Patsy" Lolordo was an organized crime figure and head of the Chicago chapter of the Unione Siciliana a front organization for the Mafia, of which Lolordo was considered one of the most powerful capos (bosses) during the late 1920s.

Lolordo dead

On January 8, 1929, Lolordo was shot and killed by unidentified gunmen in his home. The murder was arranged by Bugs Moran, a leader of the North Side Gang and a bitter rival of Capone as a preface to a planned assassination of Capone. Moran, working in concert with Aiello, was convinced that such a move would remove the bulk of Capone's Mafia protection.

The Late Tony Lombardo

A long time Mafia associate, Lombardo became Al Capone's advisor after John Torrio retired in 1925.

Lombardo (right) dead

Lombardo tried unsuccessfully to negotiate peace between the Chicago Outfit and the North Side Gang during the four-year gang war. Lombardo, with the help of Capone, later became President of the Unione Siciliana in November 1925, attempting to regain control of the unstable organization as well as instituting reforms, including opening membership to non-Sicilian Italian immigrants (such as the Neapolitan Capone) and changing the organization's name to the Italo-American National Union.

Crowd gathers around Lombardo's dead body

Lombardo's reforms, however, caused some resentment within Unione Siciliana members. With the partnership of Al Capone and New York gangster Frankie Yale worsening, possibly due to the end of payoffs from the Unione Siciliana to Yale, Lombardo would be challenged for the Presidency by Joe Aiello, supported by Yale, in January 1928.

Lombardo's wife and daughter

Lombardo, however, refused to resign and continued to organize civic projects under the Unione Siciliana until shortly before his death on September 7, 1928. Lombardo was gunned down, along with his bodyguard Joseph Ferrara (although bodyguard Joe Lolordo survived), allegedly by an alliance of the Joe Aiello Gang and the North Side Gang, at the intersections of Madison Street and Dearborn Street. It was said that Moran ordered this death and had his two experienced gunman do the job with the help of Aiello.

The Late Peg Leg Lonergan

Richard Lonergan AKA Peg Leg was a labor racketeer and high-ranking member and the final leader of the White Hand Gang. He succeeded Bill Lovett after his murder in 1923 and, under his leadership, led a two-year campaign against Frankie Yale over the New York waterfront until he and five of his lieutenants were killed in South Brooklyn during a Christmas Day celebration at the Adonis Social Club in 1925.

Lonergan was one of fifteen children, among them being Anna Lonergan known as "Queen of the Irishtown docks", born to local prize fighter and bare knuckle boxer John Lonergan. Raised in Irishtown, an Irish-American enclave between the Manhattan and Brooklyn waterfront, he later lost his right leg in a trolley car accident as a child from which his underworld nickname "Peg Leg" originated. A childhood friend and later brother-in-law of Bill Lovett, Lonergan had earned a fearsome reputation in Irishtown and on the Brooklyn waterfront as a vicious street brawler after killing a Sicilian drug dealer in a Navy Street bike shop. Believed by authorities to have been involved in at least a dozen murders during his criminal career, he was reportedly well-known for his hatred of Italian-Americans and would occasionally lead "ginzo hunting" expeditions in saloons and dive bars along the waterfront. He became the leader of the White Hand Gang shortly after the murder of its leader Bill Lovett in 1923. Lonergan spent the next two years battling Frankie Yale over control of the New York waterfront.

On the night of December 25, 1925, Lonergan and five of his men entered the Adonis Social Club during a Christmas celebration. Lonergan and the other White handers, according to witnesses, were intoxicated and being unruly to other patrons. Lonergan himself loudly and openly called nearby customers "wops", "dagos" and other ethnic slurs. When three local Irish girls entered the club escorted by their Italian dates, Lonergan chased them out supposedly yelling at them to "Come back with white men, fer chrissake!". It was at that moment that the lights went out and gunfire was heard. Customers rushed for the exits in a panic as glass was shattered as well as tables and chairs being overturned. As police arrived, they found one of Lonergan's men, his best friend Aaron Harms, dead in the street and they followed a blood trail into the club where they found Lonergan and drug addict Cornelius "Needles" Ferry on the dance floor near a player piano shot execution style. A fourth member, James Hart, managed to escape, having been found a few blocks away crawling on the sidewalk after being shot in the thigh and leg. He was taken to the Cumberland Street Hospital where he eventually recovered but refused to cooperate with police. He denied being at the club claiming he had been shot by a stray bullet by from a passing car. The two other members, Joseph "Ragtime Joe" Howard and Patrick "Happy"

Maloney, were apparently unaccounted for leaving no witnesses willing to testify. Although seven men had been arrested in connection to the shooting, including a visiting Al Capone, all the men were released on bail ranging from $5,000 to $10,000 and the case was eventually dismissed.

Anna Lonergan publicly blamed the gangland shooting on "foreigners" commenting "You can bet it was no Irish American like ourselves who would stage a mean murder like this on Christmas Day". The killings are generally attributed to Capone, in partnership with Frankie Yale, although these often colorful accounts are sometimes vague and inconsistent but allege that the incident was prearranged. It is with the death of Lonergan however that the White Hand Gang disappeared from the Brooklyn waterfront allowing Frankie Yale and eventually the Five Families to take control.

The late Mr. Lonardo

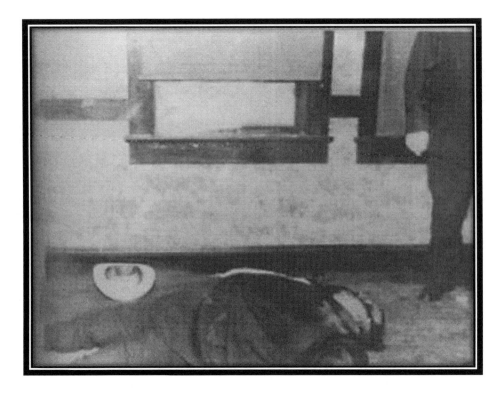

Joey Lornado, a Cleveland hood, was killed along with his brother, mob big shot Johnny Lonardo in 1927.

The late Wild Bill Lovett

After the failed attempt on his life, New York Irish gangster Bill Lovett began courting Anna Lonergan, sister of his top lieutenant Richard "Pegleg" Lonergan. After their marriage on June 26, 1923, Lovett vowed to his wife that he would not only quit drinking but to quit the criminal rackets as well. Wild Bill turned over command of the gang to new brother-in-law Pegleg Lonergan and bought a new house in Little Ferry, New Jersey. For three months, Bill Lovett managed to stay clear of trouble.

 On October 30, 1923, Bill Lovett went into New York City for the purpose of attending a job interview for the position of foreman of a silk factory. Evidently not trusting himself, he asked his wife Anna to accompany him, which she declined to do.

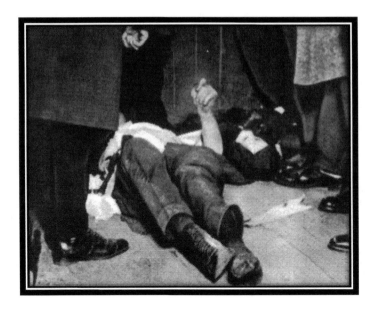

Instead of going to the interview, Wild Bill found his way back to his old haunts along the Brooklyn waterfront and began carousing with old pals. The next morning, Anna Lovett managed to track her husband to Thomas Sand's saloon. Bill got on the phone and asked his wife to come pick him up. Angry that her husband had broken his promises, Anna refused. Wild Bill stayed in the neighborhood and continued drinking, spending most of Halloween with an old friend named Joseph Flynn.

Later that night, both Flynn and Lovett staggered into the rear of an abandoned store at 25 Bridge Street to sleep off their drunks. Flynn later told police he awoke in the middle of night and went home while Lovett was still asleep.

Police later determined that sometime between 2 and 3 that morning, two men entered the rear of the store to attack Lovett. As one beat him about the head with a blunt instrument, the other shot Wild Bill three times in the head and neck. Lovett's dead body was found several hours later. He was buried in Cypress Hills Cemetery with full military honors."

While it has long been said that Wild Bill Lovett was surprised in a speakeasy and killed by gangsters working for Frankie Yale the police investigation indicated that Lovett was most probably killed by fellow Irish gangsters for one reason or another, just as his old adversary Dinny Meehan had been.

The late Mr. Magnasco

Joey Magnasco of the Gallo gang killed on 4th Avenue and Union Streets, New York 1961

The late Mrs. Mannoia

The Corleone Mafia decided to stop rats in the organization by making an example of the family of solider-turned informant Francesco Marino Mannoia. On November 23 1989, they murdered mother, the sister and an aunt.

The late Mr. Marco

Frankie Marco victim Castellmarese war

The late Mr. Maranzano

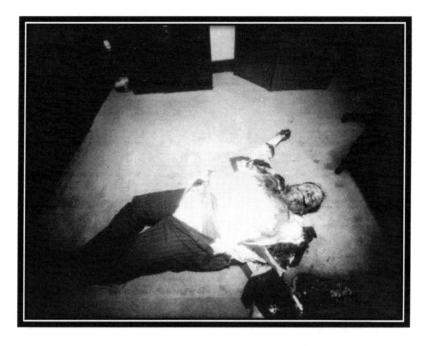

Giuseppe Masseria, AKA Joe the Boss. Masseria was the most powerful Mafia don in New York City from 1920 till 1930, with absolute control over the Lower East Side. An old world Mafia enforcer, he fled to the US from Sicily in 1903 to avoid a murder charge that even the Sicilian Mafia couldn't fix. Forced into hiding in New York, Masseria began work as an enforcer for the Morello organization, a Mafia gang, families had not yet been established in the United States, that operated on the Lower East Side, under the sponsorship of two ambitious gangsters, Iganzio Saietta and Ciro Terranova. But Masseria was equally ambitious, and after Saietta was sent to prison and Terranova retired from crime, having struck it rich by cornering the national artichoke market, Masseria, within seven years, controlled an enormous part of the rackets in New York.

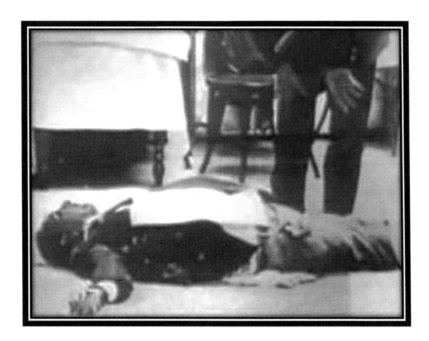

Masseria was an old world Mafia Don, a tyrannically, strict bigot, who ordered his top men, young gangsters like Charles "Lucky" Luciano, to stop associating with Jewish mobsters. It was, he said, "unwise" to have relationships outside the Sicilian organization. As for the Irish gangs that surrounded him and constantly encroached into his rackets, Masseria said it was easier to kill them than to bring them into his organization. As a result, his organization was insular and almost constantly involved in a street war.

Joe Masseria ruled supreme until 1927 when Maranzano, a native of Castellamarese del Gulfo, Sicily, came to the U.S. with permission of the Mafia Chieftain there, Cascio Ferro, with orders to bring New York under the control of the European Mafia and prepare the way for Ferro to take over. However Ferro was arrested by the Mussolini's fascists and imprisoned for life and never made it to the U.S, leaving Maranzano free reign in the United States.

Unlike most of the Mafia leaders of his time, who were crude and simple peasants, Maranzano, was a well-educated and somewhat refined former seminarian. He was also a brutal murderer who shot and stabbed his way into Masseria's rackets, causing the Castellamarese war, named after the town of Castellammare del Gulfo that spawned Maranzano and his young Americanized followers, Joe Bonanno; Jose Profaci; and Stefano Magaddino

At first, an arrogant Masseria wasn't concerned with the younger Maranzano. He responded in the old way of doing things, he filled the streets with gunmen and ordered them to kill anyone associated with the Castellamarese. While that plan may have worked in Sicily, in the new world, it failed completely largely because Masseria's men were independent business people with ongoing financial interests in prostitution; narcotics, extortion and bootleg beer and street wars were extremely expensive and took them away from the more important matters. Masseria responded by bringing in new men from Italy and paying his American crews more money as a means to keep their loyalty, but eventually his war chest started to deplete. Added to that was the fact that Masseria was extremely unpopular with his crews who were reluctant to rush into an ongoing war for a man they detested largely because he refused to share his fortunes.

At the same time, the young Turks recognized the newly arrived Maranzano as just another tyrant. The leader of the Young Turks, Charles "Lucky" Luciano, decided to kill both Masseria and Maranzano and carry through with his American vision to organize crime by ridding it of the old world mentality of the so-called "Mustache Pete's" who spent their days plotting and counter plotting old world vendettas.

Luciano had been working for Masseria but soon Maranzano learned of Luciano's talents and intelligence and was pleased when Luciano expressed an interest in switching over to his side. However, Luciano was as calculating and cunning as any old world Don and convinced Maranzano that he could turn over to his side while secretly remaining Masseria's employ as a sleeper agent.

On April 15, 1931, Luciano, with Maranzano's approval, made his move. He invited Masseria to a Coney Island restaurant, The Nuova Villa Tammaro, because Masseria knew the owner and would be comfortable there. After a meal, when the restaurant was empty of customers, Luciano excused himself and went to the bathroom. As he did this, four gunmen, Vito Genovese, Joe Adonis, Albert Anastasia, future boss of what would be the Gambino crime family and Bugsy Siegel, future builder of Las Vegas, entered the restaurant shot Masseria dead. With Masseria gone, the Castellamarese War ended with a cost of between fifty to one hundred lives.

Maranzano now declared himself Capo di tutti Capi -- or Boss of all Bosses and called for a meeting with all the Mafia members in the United States. A huge banquet hall was rented which Maranzano had decorated with religious symbols to give off an air of reverence. He addressed the meeting by explaining that his new organization would have five lieutenants below him and under them, crew chiefs, or Capo's and soldiers assigned to each "Crew" which would be made up of between 15 and 25 members of the Mafia, or "Soldiers". He further ruled that there would be no more vendetta killings and only those of Sicilian decent would be permitted to be involved in this organization.

Several days after the meeting, Maranzano began plotting the murder or his subordinates, especially Luciano. Others to be killed included Vito Genovese, future leader of the mob family that would bear his name, Al Capone of Chicago and Joe Adonis. To carry out the ghastly chore, Maranzano hired an independent Irish hoodlum named Vincent "Mad Dog" Coll.

At the same time, Luciano plotted his move against Maranzano. On September 10, 1931, six months after Masseria was killed and the same day that Maranzano had planned to have Luciano murdered, Maranzano was executed as he sat in his office. True to the new world order, Luciano sent Jewish thugs to carry out the murder. With Maranzano dead, Lucky Luciano was Boss and organized crime in America changed forever.

The late Mr. Maritote

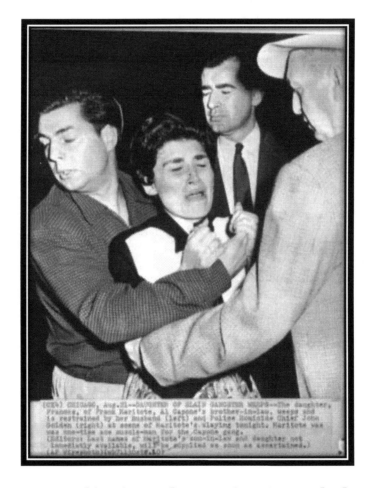

Frank Maritote, AKA Frankie Diamond, a one-time Capone bodyguard for Al Capone, had risen to become a true power in the Chicago Outfit. But then he grew old and rich and started to play things safe. He probably fingered labor goon Joey Glimco for the murder of Charlie Gioe, a co-defendants with Maritote in an extortion case. A few days later, three gunman (Probably "Milwaukee Phil"

Alderisio, Marshall Caifano, and Albert Frabotta.) pulled up in an automobile and shot Maritote to death while his infant son sat unharmed on the front seat of the car.

The late Mr. Mattarella

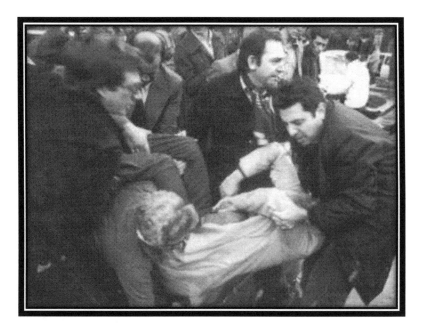

Piersanti Mattarella, a Governor in Sicily, was killed on January 6, 1980 because he promised to crack down on the mob.

The late Mrs. McErlane

Frankie McErlane "the most brutal gunman who ever pulled a trigger in Chicago." Frankie bragged that he murdered at least nine men, a woman and two dogs and is credited with introducing the Thompson sub-machine gun to Chicago's bootleg wars. McErlane's first arrest came in 1911. In June 1913, he was sent to Pontiac Prison after he was convicted of being part of an automobile theft ring. Paroled in March 1916, eight months later he would be arrested for accessory to murder in the death of an Oak Park police officer. Sent to Joliet prison, he escaped in 1918, but still served less than three years for the murder.

On May 4, 1924 McErlane was in a bar in Crown Point, Indiana drinking heavily with- John O'Reilly and Alex McCabe. When one of the men challenged him to prove his shooting prowess, McErlane pulled out his revolver and took aim at

Thaddeus S. Fancher, a local attorney having a drink at the end of the bar and fired a single bullet through the front of his head, killing him.   On January 28, 1930, McErlane was rushed to the hospital, after being shot in the right leg, above the knee, shattering the bone.   Officers who interviewed him in the emergency room didn't recognize McErlane (who was using the name Charles Miller) McErlane said that the shooting was an accident, the gun went off when he was cleaning it, a story that his common law wife, Marion Miller, backed up. Some historians hold that in fact it was Marion who fired the shots; although it's more likely the bullets came John "Dingbat" OBerta. Several nights later, McErlane was still in the hospital recovering; his leg in a plaster cast, hung in the air supported by weights and pulleys.

At around 10:30, two gunmen, probably Dingbat OBerta and Sam Malaga stood in the doorway and fired several shot at McErlane who was ready for them. He reached under his pillow where he had two loaded pistols ready and returned fire. McErlane was hit in the chest, left groin, and left wrist and the gunmen escaped, leaving behind a .45 automatic dropped which was later traced to Malaga. McErlane refused to identify the gunmen telling the police "Look for 'em in a ditch. That's where you'll find 'em. They were a bunch of cheap rats, using pistols. I'll use something better. McErlane takes care of McErlane."

 Captain John Stege ordered McErlane to be transported to Bridewell a prison hospital where police could guard him "They'll kill me if you take me out to the Bridewell." McErlane screamed. Nine days after the hospital shoot out, Dingbat OBerta and Sam Malaga, were found dead just outside the city limits, OBerta was found on the front seat of his car on the passenger side, leaning against the door, most of the top of his head gone. Malaga's body was found lying face up in an ice filled ditch. The killer had been in the car and fired from the back seat. OBerta's wife was the widow of labor racketeer, Big Tim Murphy who was murdered in June of 1928. She had Dingbat buried beside Murphy in Holy Sepulchre Cemetery, each with a rosary in their hand.

 On September 7, 1923, the Great Chicago Beer Wars began. That evening Steven, Tommy, and Walter O'Donnell, along with gangster George Bucher, George Meeghan, and Jerry O'Connor, pushed their way into a saloon run by Jacob Geis, a loyal Saltis-McErlane customer. Geis refused to carry the O'Donnells beer and was beaten senseless as a result. The brothers then made five more forays into Saltis-McErlane salon and repeated the process. It ended in a gunfight in which Jerry O'Connor, an O'Donnell gunman was killed. On September 17, McErlane responded by murdering two of O'Donnells men, Georges Bucher and George Meeghan. After that the O'Donnells backed down and the war drew to a close until the following year, 1925. Spike O'Donnell hired a few dozen gunmen and resumed his battle with the Mob. At the same time, the Saltis-McErlane gang went to war with its neighbor, the Sheldon gang. The war spilled into 1926 until the gangs called for a peace summit to be held at the Hotel Sherman on October 20. A general peace was declared and for a brief time, the shooting stopped.

  War broke out again on December 30, 1926 when Saltis gunmen killed Hilary Clements, a member of Ralph Sheldon's gang. The war eventfully ended with the near decimation of the Brother O'Donnell. McErlane's heavy drinking and his unbalanced mental state came to a head one night in September 1931, when he was found staggering drunk on 78th and Crandon Avenue, flooding the street with machine gun fire, screaming "Their after me! Don't you see them? They're laughing at me!"

A month later, on October 8, McErlane and Marion Miller were both drunk and arguing in McErlane's car when, once again, Marion, pulled a gun and fired at least one shot at McErlane but missed him. McErlane shot her dead and her two dogs as well, leaving them in the cars back seat.

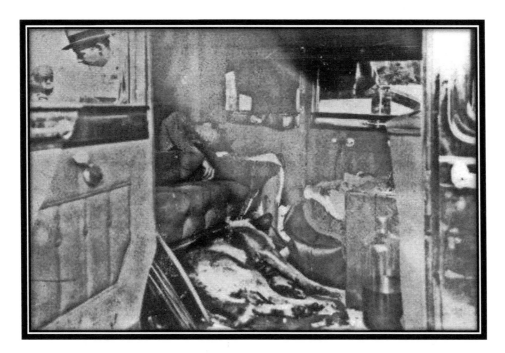

 McErlane, with at least $250,000 in cash, escaped to a houseboat on the Illinois River in Beardstown, Illinois, 200 miles southwest of Chicago. Almost exactly a year later, in October of 1932, McErlane was admitted to the Hospital in Beardstown with pneumonia. He lapsed into delirium. It took four hospital attendants to hold him down. He died on October 8, 1932, one year to the day after he murdered his wife.

The late Mr. McGurn

By 1933, Machine Gun Jack McGurn, the number one suspect in the St. Valentine's Day massacre, was broke and out of power. How broke McGurn was came through when newspaper reporters found him in a midtown restaurant and asked him if he had anything to do with the kidnapping of Jake the Barbers son, Jerome Factor. "Boys" McGurn said "I ain't made a payment on my house, the roof over my head, in 11 months, so's I guess I'm gonna lose the place to foreclosure. So if I snatched Jake's kid, believe you me, I would have collected the dough long before this"

Three years later, Jack McGurn went down to Florida and begged Willie Heeney, a pimp and drug addict under Capone, but a power in the labor extortion business, to set up a meeting between him, the Mobs banker, Jake Guzak and Nitti. In the old days, Heeney would have told the world that one of Capone's top sluggers was interested in talking to him.

Now it was different. At the age of 33 McGurn's world had fallen apart. The Saint Valentine's Day murders had made him too hot for the syndicate to deal with. His gorgeous wife, Louis, "The Blonde Alibi" he had used to keep him from being convicted for his role in the Massacre by testifying they were holed up in a love nest at the time of the shooting, left him years ago when his money ran because of his gambling problem.

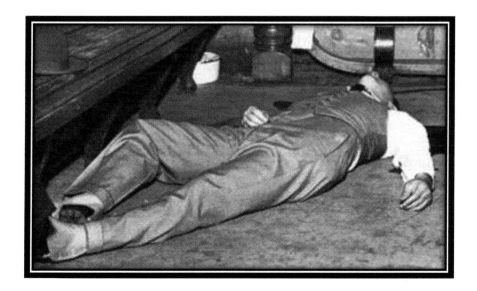

Now McGurn was reduced to running numbers and selling junk, dope, in the Black neighborhoods. But he wasn't much good at that either. McGurn was never an "earner", a money hustler; he was an enforcer, a pretty boy killer, with a mean streak. But, with Capone gone and the beer wars over, McGurn was of no use to anyone anymore. And a lot of hatred towards him from inside the Mob was personal.

As McGurn went down the in the ranks, the hoods that had been on the lower end of the chain, like Heeney, were rising up and they delighted in abusing the once arrogant McGurn, now that Capone wasn't around to protect him. Now, in 1936, when the Mob was on the brink of earning more money than it ever dreamed of, Machine Gun Jack McGurn had to beg for a five-minute appointment to see Heeney, Guzak and Nitti. In the meeting, held on a golf course outside Miami,

McGurn said that he needed a job inside Nitti's loan sharking operation. They turned him down. He was high profile and the stigma of the massacre never left him. In desperation, McGurn launched into a plan he had of running dope from the Caribbean into Chicago to flood the Black neighborhoods. If the bosses would front the money, McGurn swore, his plan would make them all rich.

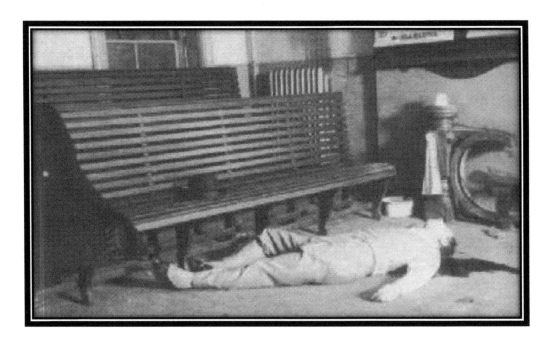

That's how far down the ladder McGurn was. He didn't know Nitti was already working with Lucky Luciano to establish dope routes in California and Florida. McGurn was dismissed and told to return to Chicago. He was all done in the rackets as far as they were concerned.

In 1936, the evening before Saint Valentine's Day, Machine Gun Jack McGurn went bowling at a second floor alley at 805 Milwaukee Avenue. (Still standing, it has been a warehouse for many decades since the murder) Three men walked in and stood behind his chair. One of them said "Stick em up and stand where you are." Nobody knows who the three men were.

Years later, Tony Accardo said he had been in the group, but as Accardo's power grew, and fewer and fewer people questioned his tales, The Accardo had a tendency to put himself virtually everywhere in Mob history including his claim that he was one of the gunmen at the massacre. While that doesn't seem likely, there is some evidence that Accardo and other member of his Alma Mata, the Circus Gang, did plan the massacre. One of the three killers whispered to McGurn "This is for you, you son a bitch" and then aimed a pistol carefully just below McGurn's right ear, and then fired a volley into the McGurn. Then he fired another round into his lower neck.

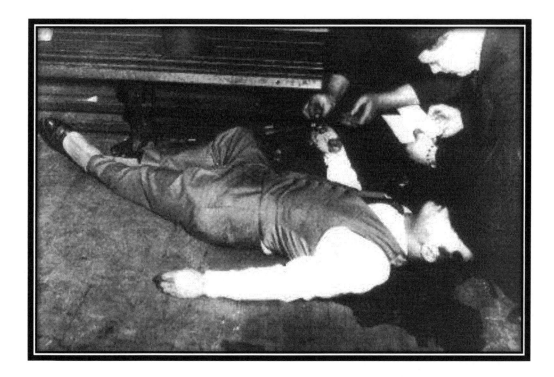

The pool hall owner, oddly enough named Tony Accardo, watched the first bullet enter McGurn, and then leaped for the floor and rolled under a pool table, and then watched the men carefully stretch out McGurn's body on the alley way and leave a card on his chest that showed a man and women without clothes on, staring at a sign that read "House for sale."

   The card read
"You lost your job"
"You lost your dough
"Your Jewels and Handsome Houses"
"But things could be much worse you know"
"You could have lost your trousers"

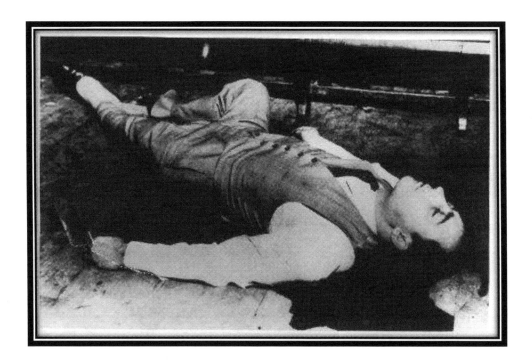

Before the killers left, one of them turned and walked back to the table where McGurn had been sitting just a minute before, and took the tally sheet which had the names of McGurn's bowling partners on it, shoved it in his pocket and walked away into the night. The police found $3.85 in his pockets. There was no life insurance policy, but somehow the family managed to have him buried in a $1,000.00 copper coffin. His three younger brothers carried him to his grave, while McGurn's mother wailed "Why! Why did they kill my boy? He never did anything to anybody!"

Police search McGurn's car for clues

Al Capone, jailed at Alcatraz, sent a dozen white roses. Sixteen days later, on March 2, perhaps remembering the families tradition for vengeance, the Mob hunted down McGurn's younger brother and former bodyguard, Anthony, to a local pool hall where he was playing cards and cut him to pieces with a rifle. Nobody will ever know who killed McGurn or why. The popular theory was that Bugs Moran had done the deed, but that doesn't seem likely.

The late Mr. McPadden

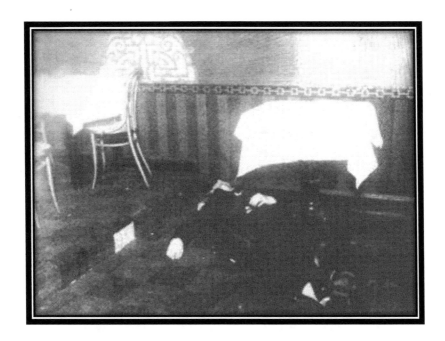

Gangster Billy "Gunner" McPadden was gunned down on New Year's Eve 1929 for crossing sides during a gang war

The late Mr. McSwiggin

William McSwiggin was Assistant State's Attorney in Chicago, and had vigorously pursued an indictment against Al Capone for the 1924 for killing Joe Howard. Working with the press. Mc Swiggin built up a repitation as Chicago hanging prosecutor.

That was one side of him, The side was that most of McSwiggin's plas were hoodlums and even Al Capone came to consider him a close personnel friend. One night in 1926, McSwiggin went out drinking with the O'Donnell brothers, rival bootleggers who had a growing feud with Capone.

They landed at the Pony Inn, not far from Capone's Cicero headquarters. When Capone learned that his rivals were in the neighborhood he sent a convoy of shooters by the Pony Inn to investigate.

As McSwiggin and the others left the Pony Inn, bursts of gunfire sent fifty rounds into the group, killing three, including McSwiggin.

The late Vern Miller

 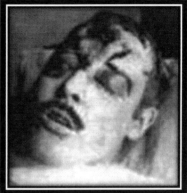

On November 29, 1933, Miller's body was found in a roadside ditch outside Detroit Michigan. He had been beaten and strangled to death. Although the cause of Miller's death remains unclear, probable causes include retaliation for the murder of Zwillman's gang member one month earlier, punishment for the failure of the Kansas City Massacre, and perhaps retribution for the Fox Lake Massacre

The late Miss Monroe

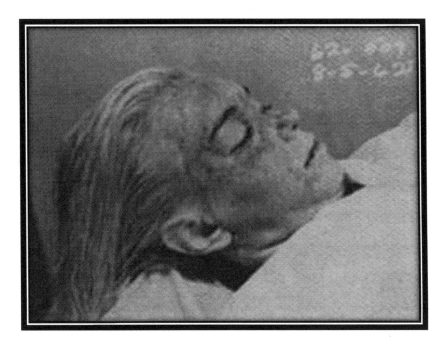

Did the mob kill Marilyn Monroe with a deadly injection?

The late Mr. Moran

 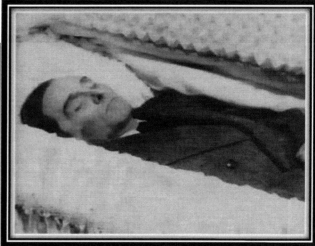

Boss Shannon views Bugs body in 1954

Bugs Moran, who survived the St. Valentine's Day Massacre by simply not being there, died of cancer in prison Feburary 25, 1957. His final days in gangland were as miserable as Capone's or McGurn's. When prohibition ended, Moran's money was gone. In July of 1946, he robbed a bank with a group of small time hoods. They got $10,000.00, a paltry sum that he once would have scoffed at. Arrested and convicted in the robbery, he died in his sleep and is buried on the prison grounds in an unmarked pauper's grave.

The late Mr. Moretti

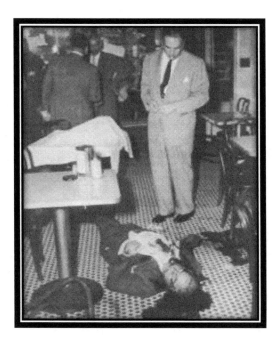

On October 4, 1951 the Mafia killed New Jersey boss Willie Moretti. Moretti was suffering from syphilis and had begun to act strange. And it all came clear when he appeared before the Kefauver committee. Boss Vito Genovese knew, Moretti was also a womanizer who had a liking for low-cost prostitutes, the darker and the younger, the better. Eventually, he developed syphilis, which went untreated and began to advance to the gangster mind and into his nervous system. He began to act strangely, doing and saying things that troubled the underworld, especially now that he had been called before the Kefauver committee.

Under oath, Moretti admitted that he was a gambler, that he knew Costello, Genovese and Adonis and every other big name gangster in the country and, further, that he was proud of those associations. He finished his testimony by inviting the committee to visit him at his home down on the Jersey shore. After that, he became something of a media celebrity, holding spur of the moment press conferences, giving reporters his opinion about the state of the world and even how to curb the growing power of the mob. Moretti was becoming an embarrassment to Costello and a minor danger to what would become the Genovese family. Vito Genovese saw the opening he was looking for. He quietly and cunningly began to spread rumors within the family and the ever-paranoid mob, that Willie Moretti was a security risk for everyone and said that Frank Costello was wrong to protect Moretti. But the real reason Genovese wanted Moretti dead, aside from ruining Costello's position within the family, was to take control of his lucrative gambling assets, a move he had readied for by positioning one of his best men, Jerry Catena, to take over as soon as Moretti was killed. With control of the gambling rackets, Genovese would have enough money to fight Costello for control of the family.

Willie Moretti outside the Kefauver hearings, joking with the press. The appearance cost him his life

Frank Costello fought it, but the National Commission approved Willie Moretti's execution. At nine a.m. on October 4, 1951, Albert Anastasia, who lived in Fort Lee, New Jersey, telephoned Moretti at his home and said that he had back troubles, and needed to go for x-rays but his chauffeur wasn't available. He asked if he could use Harry Shepherd, Moretti's driver and ever-faithful bodyguard. Moretti agreed. Later that morning, Moretti, alone and unarmed, drove to Joe's

Elbow Room Restaurant in suburban Cliffside, New Jersey, where three men were waiting for him. Moretti joined them at their table and the group spoke in Italian. Suddenly one of the men drew a revolver and shot Willie Moretti twice in the forehead, leaving his body sprawled on the patterned linoleum, between two tables.

Murder Inc.

Murder Incorporated was largely but no exclusively a Jewish operation, the group of professional killers was actually called, inside the criminal world at the time, The Brownsville Boys or "Lepke's (Buchalter) group" A reporter named Harry Feeny, who wrote for the New York World-Telegram is generally credited with making up the name Murder Incorporated.

It probably is not true that the gang was kept on by the national syndicate to enforce its will in the underworld anywhere in the United States. It is more likely that the group was simply a lose formation of hoodlums who riled over the Brooklyn garment industry by gun and knife, killing their competitors and other assorted persons who caused them trouble.

Members of the group included Abe "Kid Twist" Reles, Frank "Dasher" Abbandando, Louis Capone, Martin "Buggsy" Goldstein, Harry "Happy" Maione, Harry "Pittsburgh Phil" Strauss, Allie Tannenbaum, Seymour "Blue Jaw" Magoon, and Charles "Charlie the Bug" Workman, Louis "Lepke" Buchalter, Harry "Pittsburgh Phil" Strauss, Louis Capone, Allie Tannenbaum, Mendy Weiss, Irving "Knadles" Nitzberg, Vito "Socko" Gurino, Jacob "Jack" Drucker,

Sholom Bernstein and Philip "Little Farvel" Cohen. Almost all the members of the group hailed from the Brownsville section of Brooklyn or from the general area of East New York.

The group arranged the murder of Dutch Schultz and his men on October 23, 1935, in the Palace Chop House in Newark, New Jersey. The murder, done by Charles Workman and Mendy Weiss, was done for a fee and probably killed others, usually informant, such as loan shark George Rudnick who was cut into pieces by the gangsters, for fees as well. The price for murders ranged from $1,000 to $5,000. But in all likelihood, the gang conducted no more or no less killings than any other mob in New York and most of their killings took place in Brooklyn. It is very unlikely that gang killed anywhere near the 1000 people legend has credited with.

The beginning of the end for the gang started in January of 1940, when Harry "Harry the Mock" Rudolph, a life-long criminal and police informer sent a handwritten note to Brooklyn District Attorney William O'Dwyer. At the time, Rudolph was being held in the city jail at Rikers Island as a material witness in the 1933 murder of Alex "Red" Alpert in Brooklyn. (Born 1933)

Alpert, only twenty years old, was a burglar with a long history of arrests. On November 25, 1933, he was found dead in a courtyard at 390 Van Siclen Avenue in Brooklyn. (Reles would later give his address as 427 Van Siclen) Known as a brawler with a hair trigger temper, Alpert was out on bail for assaulting two policemen. He had been shot to death.

The note, on prison stationary, read

"Dear Sir:

I am doing a bit here. I would like to talk to the District Attorney. I know something about a murder in East New York."

Harry Rudolph

Rudolph was largely considered to be mentally unbalanced but O'Dwyer's office had no choice but to investigate, it was after all, a murder charge. Rudolph was very clear to the investigators, he would give solid information in exchange for a considerations in the future.

He then told investigators that he was friends with Alpert and he knew for a fact that Abe Reles, Martin Buggsy Goldstein and Anthony Dukey Maffetore (Also known as The Duke) had murdered Alpert on orders of Pittsburgh Phil Strauss. According to Rudolph, Alpert had robbed some jewels and tried to fence them with Strauss, who was always flush with cash. The two men could not agree on a price and the young and quick-tempered Alpert left in a huff after insulting Strauss. Rudolph said he witness the killing and would testify to as much in court.

Anthony Maffetore was picked up by police first while Reles and Goldstein turned themselves in the next morning. It was Reles 44th arrest since 1933 (Six of them for murder) and Goldstein's 34th arrest (Four of them for murder)

It should have been a standard arrested but back on Riker's Island, a conman named Abraham Frosch, (Born 1915. He lived at 1515 East Twenty-Seventh Street in Brooklyn) speaking for Reles and Goldstein offered Harry Rudolph $5,000 in cash to pin the murder on Duke Maffetore and "To put Reles and Goldstein on the street"

O'Dwyer's office left no time in telling Duke Maffetore about the bribe and how Reles and Goldstein planned to have the murder pinned on him. Maffetore immediately turned the tables and agreed to cooperate with the law. He said that he was no in on the Alpert killing but he had been the driver on at least six other murders. O'Dwyer would need him because on June 4, 1940, Harry Rudolph, O'Dwyer's informant, died in the hospital on Rikers Island of natural causes.

The danger in Maffetore's testimony was that it was clear that he was fringe player in the organization and not a killer. O'Dwyer told him to bring in a cooberating witness and Maffetore convinced Abraham "Pretty" Levine to work with the government since Levine, like Maffetore, was going to be indicted for his role in stealing a car that used in a murder. (Charges against Maffetore and Levine were later reduced. In Levine's case, his wife was also tossed in jail on a trumpet up charge to add pressure to Levine to get him to agree to testify)

 Levine was a 26 year old who looked more like a schoolboy, was a suspect in at least six gangland murders. Recently married and the father of a newborn, he was a truck driver by profession but had borrowed money from Pittsburgh Phil Strauss to help make end meet and Strauss dragged him further and further into the underworld. (He also charged him 20% interest on the loan he had to him) With his wife's urging, Levine talked.

 He implicated Pittsburgh Phil Strauss, Happy Maione, Dasher Abbandando, Louis Capone, Buggsy Goldstein and Kid Twist Reles in a dozen murders. He confirmed that Strauss, Reles, Louis Capone and Buggsy Goldstein had murdered Red Alpert. He also told O'Dwyer about the murder of Walter Sage, a Brooklyn bookie had had been skimming money from the gangs slot machine business. Pittsburgh Phil and Jack Drucker, strangled Sage, used an ice pick on him, tied his corpse to a pinball machine which then dumped into a Catskill Mountain lake.

The next to break was, surprisingly, Abe Reles himself. Reles realized that someone was talking to O'Dwyer, someone from the inside, and that he had the most to lose since he had committed most of the gang's murders.

Reles, who had a pronounced lisp and bad personnel hygiene, had a remarkably long police record, but few convictions. Arrested for the murder of Red Alpert, Reles sat in a cell in the Tombs, a dreary, dangerous Manhattan jail and considered his option and the best option he had was to try and cut a deal. He sent his wife to O'Dwyer's office to work out the details. When Reles began to talk, he talked to two weeks and gave details on 85 gangland murders in Brooklyn. He also detailed the inner workings of the national syndicate, an organization that virtually no one had ever heard of before.

When they learned that Reles was cooperating, Albert Tannenbaum, Seymour Magoon and Sholem Bernstein, all gang members, agreed to cooperate as well. Harry Maione and Frank Abbandando were gang members to be placed on trial, in May of 1940, for the 1936 murder of George Rudnick in a Brooklyn parking garage. Harry Strauss was also indicted for the Rudnick murder but he agreed to cooperate with the state and was severed from the trial. Abe Reles testified that Strauss claimed that Rudnick was an informant and should be killed.

Reles said that Maione, Abbandando and Strauss went into Rudnick's office and stabbed him to death with an ice pick. Reles said he waited outside of the garage with Angelo "Julie" Catalano, and waited for Strauss to call him in to move the body. Reles said when he saw Rudnick, he was bloody but still alive until Strauss started to jam his ice pick into Rudnick until he was certain he was dead. Then Maione used a meat cleaver on him to be absolutely sure he was dead.

On May 23, 1940, Maione and Abbandando were convicted of first-degree murder, a charge that brought a mandatory death sentence in the electric chair. They were both executed in Sing-Sing prison in 1942.

Pittsburgh Phil Strauss and Buggsy Goldstein were put on trial for the September 4, 1939 strangulation murder of bookmaker Irving Puggy Feinstein. (Born 1910. He lived at 1437 Forty-Seventh Street in Brooklyn) Feinstein had made the mistake of lending loan shark money to some of the gangs better customers. For that, he was knifed to death, set on fire and left in a vacant lot.

At this point, Strauss decided that the only way not to be executed was to feign insanity. It didn't work. On September 19, 1940, Strauss and Goldstein were convicted of first-degree murder and were executed in the electric chair at Sing-Sing on June 12th, 1941.

Next, O'Dwyer indicted gang member Charles Charlie the Bug Workman for the Dutch Schultz murders. Workman was extradited to New Jersey, found guilty and sent to prison for two decades. Then Irving "Knaldes" Nitzberg was tried for the murder of Albert Plug Shuman, a police informant, in Brooklyn, on January 9, 1939. Nitzberg shot Shuman twice in the back of the head. Nitzberg was found guilty (Twice) but the conviction was overturned by a higher court.

Lepke, Weiss, Louis Capone and Philip Little Farvel Cohen were indicted for the murder of Joe Rosen in Brooklyn on September 13, 1936. They were found guilty and executed on March 4, 1944.

Vito Socko Gurino confessed to three murders and implicated himself in four others. In April 1942, Gurino was sentenced to 80 years-to-life in prison.

Jacob Jack Drucker and Irving Big Gangi Cohen, were tried for the murder of Walter Sage. Witnesses said that Cohen had stabbed Sage with an ice pick 36 times. He was acquitted

Drucker was convicted of second-degree murder on May 5, 1944 and received a sentence of 25 Years-to-Life. He died in Attica prison in January 1962.

Max "the "Jerk" Golob was indicted with Frank Abbandando for first-degree murder in the slaying of gangster John Spider Murtha on March 3, 1935. It was a weak case and they were permitted to plead down the charges.

Jack "The "Dandy" Parisi was acquitted of murdering Teamsters official Morris Diamond music-publishing executive Irving Penn (Penn was killed in a tragic case of by mistaken-identity)

The end came for Reles on November 12, 1941 when he was more than likely tossed out the window of his room at the Half Moon Hotel on Coney by the five policemen assigned to protect him.

By 1952, nothing remained of Murder Incorporated. Philip "Little Farvel" Cohen was murdered in 1949, after his release from prison. Anthony "The "Duke" Maffetore, vanished on March 7, 1951 and is presumed murdered. Seymour "Blue Jaw" Magoon, who had also testified against the gang, vanished and is believed to have lived out his life Bridgeport Connecticut under the name Mulligan.

As for Abraham Frosch, the man who offered Rudolph the bribe, in 1943 he was sentenced to five years in prison for running a fake lottery. In August of 1963, Frosch, then running a motel in the Catskills, was arrested with a dozen others, for running a $13 million dollar a year bookie operation in the resort area.

The late Mr. Navara

Michele Navarra was boss of the Corleone based Mafia family until he was murdered on August 2nd 1958 by Luciano Leggio who replaced him as head of the family.

The late Mr. Oberta

Chicago's Digbat Oberta

Oberta bodyguard, Sammy Malaga probably spotted the killers coming and leaped into the back seat of the car. At the last minute he made a run for ti but was gunned down, His body was later recovered from under the ice.

The late Mr. O'Hare

Edward J. O'Hare, no one ever called him Edward, it was Eddie, was a lawyer from St. Louis. Early in his career, he entered a partnership with a local inventor named Oliver P. Smith, who in 1909 had developed a mechanical rabbit for use in dog racing. Over the next decade, Smith refined his invention and O'Hare took out the patent. Together, they toured the country and showed the running rabbit system, just as the sport of dog racing was catching on. With time, they had great success, taking a percentage of the gate in exchange for use of their invention

When the inventor died in 1927, O'Hare, the lawyer, cheated Smith's wife out of any rights she had to the invention, gained complete control of the rights to the rabbit for himself.

Flush with cash, Fast Eddie O'Hare dumped his long suffering wife, took his three children, Butch and his sisters Patricia and Marilyn, and moved to Chicago.

Like almost everyone else who met him, Al Capone took an immediate liking to Eddie O'Hare, and brought him into Hawthorne Kennel Club, a Cicero dog race track, as a major partner.

Dog racing was illegal in Illinois, but O'Hare and the boys kept the place open by successfully tying up its opponents in court for decades.

It was worth the costs of the lawyers too, because O'Hare figured out a way to fix the races. He fed seven of the eight dogs in the race a greasy hamburger just minutes before the race was to begin, and then placed the mob's money on the unfed dog.

O'Hare and Capone made so much money from the Hawthorne scam, that they were able to open tracks in Boston and Florida.

When the law finally shut down the Hawthorne as a dog track, the hoods quickly converted it into the Sportsman's Park Race Track and began to run thoroughbred horses there, with O'Hare as its President. In the off season, Fast Eddie kept himself busy by setting up tax dodging real estate deals and the occasional political payoff.

But, while Fast Eddie O'Hare might have failed as a human being, he was a better than average father, doting on his children, and sprinkling every conversation with his favorite "My son, Butch."

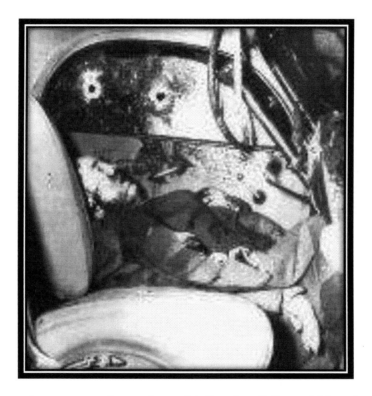

When Butch was about to graduate from high school, he told his father that he wanted to go to the US Naval Academy at Annapolis, which required the backing of a local representative in Congress. At the same time, Capone was locked in the midst of his tax fight with the government, which was desperately trying to put Capone away.

It so happened that one day Eddie O'Hare ran into a reporter from the St. Louis Post Dispatch named John Rogers, who was also a friend of one of the prosecutors going after Capone.

Rogers knew that O'Hare wanted to get his son into Annapolis. Introductions were made and a deal was cut, Butch O'Hare would enter Annapolis if Eddie O'Hare would play ball with the government and inform on Capone, which he did and did well.

Capone went away forever, Frank Nitti took over the outfit and Eddie O'Hare went on to make even more money at various mob related ventures.

In 1935, he purchased the Chicago Cardinals Football Club, and expanded his real estate holding to southern California. Life was good. O'Hare fell in love with his secretary, Ursula Sue Granata, sister of a Mobbed State Representative. The engagement went on for seven years because, as Catholics, O'Hare's divorce from his wife made it impossible for the couple to have a church wedding, and Sue Granata wanted a church wedding. However, Eddie had spread around some cash, and he was hopeful that a request for a dispensation from the Vatican would come through by 1940.

In the meantime, Fast Eddie never did stop informing on the mobsters he did business with, but, unlike the legend that has grown up around him, O'Hare didn't inform on the mob for altruistic reasons, he did it for the money. Anytime a mob partner would lean on him for a higher percentage or cheat him out of a dollar, Fast Eddie O'Hare would drop a dime on the thug.

It was a great deal for Fast Eddie, or at least it was until the day he cheated Paul Ricca, the reigning mob boss at the time, out of his fair share of a deal they had worked together.

Ricca took his justice on November 8, 1939. That day, O'Hare was seen cleaning and loading a Spanish-made .32-caliber semi-automatic pistol in his office at Sportsman's Park. He left his office that afternoon, got into his black 1939 Lincoln coupe, and drove away from the track.

As Fast Eddie approached the intersection of Ogden and Rockwell, a car roared up beside him and two shotgun-wielding punks opened up on him with a volley of big-game slugs. O'Hare was killed instantly. Inside the car, Police found the gun that O'Hare never had a chance to use. It was in his coat pocket next to a rosary, a crucifix, a religious medallion and a poem clipped from a magazine. The poem read: "The clock of life is wound but once And no man has the power To tell just when the hands will stop At late or early hour. Now is the only time you own. Live, love, toil with a will. Place no faith in time. For the clock may soon be still."

Edward Butch O'Hara

As was his father's wish, Butch O'Hare graduated from the Naval Academy at Annapolis, Maryland in 1937. When war broke out with Japan, he was shipped off to the Gilbert Islands in the Pacific to fly a single-engine Grumman F4F fighter.

One day, while flying a mission, O'Hare, accompanied by a wingman in another Grumman Hellcat, spotted nine Japanese twin-engine bombers zeroing in on the aircraft carrier Lexington.

O'Hare zoomed in to attack the Japanese fighters when the .50 caliber machine guns in the second Grumman jammed, leaving only O'Hare between the airborne assassins and the USS Lexington.

O'Hare attacked the superior enemy force, alone, flying straight into their formation, guns blazing. One by one, he picked them off, downing five of the nine Japanese attackers. Three more were shot down by Lexington pilots who were able to take off after O'Hare first engaged the bombers and the last Japanese plane, badly damaged in the shootout with O'Hare, crashed at sea some distance away.

O'Hare was designated the Navy's first Ace of World War II. He was immediately promoted two grades from Lieutenant Junior Grade to Lieutenant Commander and President Roosevelt called his outstanding performance, "One of the most daring, if not the most daring, single action in the history of combat aviation."

On November 26, 1943, while on a night interception near Tarawa, Butch O'Hare was shot down and lost at sea. There is one last footnote to this story. Several months after Eddie was gunned down, Frank Nitti, the boss who ordered his murder, married Ursula Sue Granata, O'Hare's fiancée.

The late Mr. Panto

Peter Panto was that he was a self-appointed labor leader on the Brooklyn waterfront, perhaps a communist, and was effective enough to raise the anger of the Mafia boss Albert Anastasia. Burton B. Turkus, who had been Assistant District Attorney for Kings County (Brooklyn), wrote "In mid-summer 1939," Turkus and Feder wrote, "Peter Panto was waging a determined war against gangster rule on the water front. For months, he had been whipping up the longshoremen to shake off the mobster grip. Panto was only twenty-eight... 'We are strong,' he urged the union men. 'All we have to do is stand up and fight. 4
 Panto's fate was sealed after he called a meeting of ILA local 929 on July 8, 1939, attended by 1,250 members, where Panto's insisted on an honest election for the local. The Longshoremen stood to their feet and cheered him as the Mafia's enforcers looked on, stupefied.

On Friday July 14, Panto was visiting his fiancée, who bore the unfortunate surname Maffia. At 10 p.m., there was a knock on the door. Panto answered it and then stepped outside to talk to two men. According to Organized Crime contract killer Abe Reles, the men insisted that Panto's come with them to meet union officials who wanted to offer him cash to leave the docks. When Panto's refused, he was beaten, tossed into a car and driven to an isolated spot. Although Panto's was slight in build, weighing less than 163 pounds, he fought the gangsters and according to Reles, nearly biting off the finger of killer Mendy Weiss before he could be overpowered and strangled to death. He was covered in quicklime and buried in a New Jersey lot.

The late Mr. Pisano

"Little Augie" Pisano

On the night of September 25, 1959 New York gangster Anthony Strollo invited Little Augie Carfano to dinner at Marino's restaurant and Carfano accepted. Earlier that night Carfano relaxed at the famous Copacabana nightclub and later that evening left to meet with Strollo. At Marino's, Carfano ran into mutual friends among them Janice Drake, a former Miss New Jersey and the wife of comedian Alan Drake. Drake had been previously called in as a witness to testify on gangland slayings of Manhattan Nathan Nelson and Gambino crime family boss Albert Anastasia. Carfano offered to drive Janice home after supper to her apartment in Rego Park, Queens where her 13-year old son Michael was sleeping.

In the middle of the meal, Carfano allegedly received a phone call. After hanging up, Carfano told his group that he and Drake had to leave; he had been called away "on urgent business". Carfano and Drake left Marino's and drove away in his Cadillac. Police later theorized that this phone call was from Costello warning Carfano about the hit. When Carfano and Drake left the restaurant, they were allegedly heading to La Guardia Airport in Queens to board a flight to Miami. However, according to this theory, Strollo had anticipated such a move and had hidden gunmen in the back seat of the Cadillac. Once on the road, the gunmen forced Carfano to drive to a quiet location near the airport. At 10:30 that evening, 45 minutes after Carfano and Drake left Marino's, their bodies were found in Carfano's car near the airport. Both had been shot in the back of the head.

Another theory regarding Carfano's death lies with his vast gambling empire in South Florida and a belief he was making moves to investment in Cuban casinos at the time of his death. With the emergence of Genovese as the new leader of the Luciano crime family in late 1957, former boss Luciano lost a great deal of underworld influence in New York and America. No longer in control of his crime family, longtime Luciano ally and supporter Meyer Lansky who had vast gambling interests across America, along with casino interests in Las Vegas and Cuba was in need of a new sponsor and ally within the former Luciano family. Luciano and Costello had given Lansky underworld protection for decades. Now Lansky sought an alliance with new boss Vito Genovese.

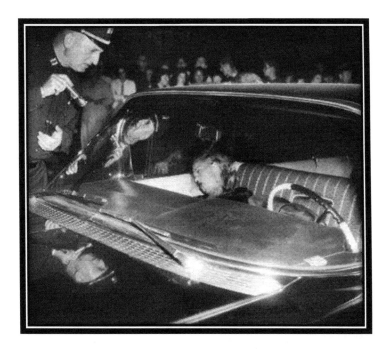

Underworld rumor has it that after Costello was deposed as boss of the Luciano crime family in late 1957, Carfano took it upon himself to show much disregard and even contempt for the new leadership. He apparently spent most of his time overseeing his criminal and legitimate interests South Florida and traveled to New York only when necessary, and by 1959 had begun making plans to expand his gambling operations into Cuba. The theory goes that Carfano, who was not a Genovese supporter began to encroach on the Havana casino operations of Meyer Lansky and the new Genovese crime family.

With Carfano's prior, blatant disrespect for his new boss Genovese and now his encroachment onto Genovese and Lansky territory without permission sealed Carfano's fate. This, along with the added bonus that Lansky would take over all the Carfano gambling interests in Florida where Lansky was also based gave the two New York Mob bosses all the excuse they needed to have Carfano hit that fateful September night. The fact that Lansky's criminal association with Genovese strengthened after his takeover of the Luciano crime family and that Lansky did in fact take over Carfano's Southern Florida gambling interests after his death is more than likely the catalyst for this theory surrounding Carfano's murder and Lansky's involvement

The late Mr. Petrocelli

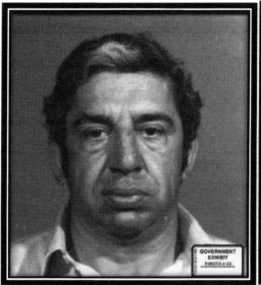 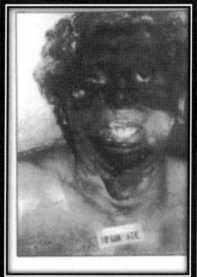

William "Butch" Petrocelli was a feared killer who got on the wrong side of the Chicago Outfit so they decied to kill him. Angelo "The Hook" LaPietra was the set him up, sending him down the block from a Chinatown social club where killer Nicholas Calabrese waited. Calabrese told of the murder

"It happened so fast, he was on the ground," Nicholas Calabrese testified."I remember holding him down, and my brother choking him" Helping in killing Petrocelli was Jimmy LaPietra and Frank Santucci. Waiting in cars nearby were Frank Furio and Johnny "Apes" Monteleone.

Calabrese cut Petrocelli's throat. It was a pattern with him; strangle the victim then cut his throat, just to make sure the the victim was dead. He then burned Petrocelli's corpse using two big cans of Zippo lighter fluid.

The late Porrello Brothers

Raymond and Rosario Porrello, murder 1932

On July 5, 1930 Cleveland hood Joe Porrello was contacted by his enemy Frank Milano and invited to a sitdown at the Milano owned Venetian to discuss business affairs and peaceful solution to the conflicts erupting between the two top Cleveland Mafia factions. Joe Porrello and his bodyguard arrived for the meeting and soon gunfire erupted and both Porrello gang members, leader Joe Porrello and his underling were dead. On August 15, 1930, just three weeks after the murder of brother Vincenzo, a violent explosion leveled Raymond Porrello's home, but luckily he was not home at the time. By this time the Mayfield Road Mob and its leaders had taken over the Cleveland Mafia with the backing of various New York Mafia bosses and the Porrellos were effectively no longer an underworld power in Cleveland.

The Last of the Purple Gang

The Purples were primarily a prohibition era gang active in Detroit.

The undisputed leader was Sammy "Purple" Cohen who joined his gang with the Oakland Sugarhouse gang under the direction of the Bernstein brothers, Abe, Ray and Joe. Together they were transformed from a small time gang of troublesome teens to bootleggers and occasional muscle for other, larger bootleg gangs.

Author Paul Kavieff, who has written extensively about the gang said

"The Purples were, for the most part, the sons of recently immigrated Russian Jews, although some of the members were actually born in the old country and brought here as infants, all of them were the sons of the working poor. The Purples were really a very loose confederation of mostly, but not exclusively,

Jewish gangsters. Well, the gang started as a group of juvenile delinquents on the lower east side of Detroit, a group of about 16 or 17 children from the same neighborhood. Mostly they were involved in the usual petty crime of juveniles, rolling drunks and stealing from hucksters. It was the advent of prohibition that really got them organized, prohibition started in Michigan on May 1, 1918.

Detroit was really the first US City with a population of over 250,000 to have a prohibition law. The opportunities provided by that, early prohibition, are what helped to escalate these kids into mobsters. Remember, Detroit is a mile away from Windsor, Canada and beer was easily available there from their export docks.

Strangely, Ontario, where Windsor is, had a prohibition law but not a law against exporting liquor to countries that didn't have prohibition, so just about anybody with a rowboat could go over there, and tell the export people they were picking up a shipment that was to go to Cuba. Nobody asked a lot of questions.

The money was fantastic. By 1923, the bootleg business in Detroit was estimated to be over $250,000,000 a year, but the Purples weren't so much involved in bootlegging liquor as they were hijacking liquor and that was really how they made their reputation.

They were a predatory group and they were known for their ruthlessness, I mean they shoot everybody during these hijackings, even the guys who were simply driving the trucks. What that resulted in was that if you were making a beer delivery and were robbed by the Purples, you fought to the death, because you knew that the Purples were going to haul you out of the truck and kill you anyway. By 1925, the Purples had established themselves as strong-arm guys, bodyguards and the like, for gamblers in Detroit.

"There isn't a lot of available to clearly explain the origins of the name, but it was probably a journalistic adventure because I found no reference to any operation called the Purple Gang until 1928. One story was that when they were kids and were stealing from shopkeepers, one of the shopkeepers said that "those kids are off-colored, they're purple, purple like the color of bad meat."

Another story is that there had been two brothers, Sam and Ben Purple, who had been associated with the gang when they were juveniles, but had nothing to do with the adult organized crime group. But I don't believe that has anything to do with it. Again, my best guess is that the name was a media invention. The core group of the gang was composed of the Bernstein brothers, Abe and Joe, who were the leaders of the gang. Abe was more or less the diplomat Joe was the mover and shaker on the street. He later became a legitimate businessman. The core was ten or twelve guys who grew up on the lower east side of Detroit. Sometimes the gang numbered as high as eighteen or slightly more.

The Purples did sell drugs, actually I should say, what they did was to create a protection racket for the hoods who did sell drugs as a main source of income. So a dealer could operate in the city and make a lot of money selling drugs in so long as they kicked back to the Purple Gang, if they didn't kick back to the Purples, then the Purples brutally put them out of business. The same was true for the Handbook industry. Once there was one Handbook operator who refused to pay the Purples so they took him and brought him out to the Lake, cut a hole in it and dunked him in the ice a couple of times, after that, he paid.

The so-called Little Jewish Navy was a fraction of the Purple Gang and was led by a guy named One Armed Gelfin. Gelfin and several others in the group were Chicago gangsters who were thrown out of Chicago by the Capone mob, were the core of the group. Again, there were about ten or twelve members in all.

They were bankrolled in this venture by the Purples. The group also did enforcement work for the Purples too. Otherwise, they had about a dozen fast boats and they hauled liquor from Canada into Detroit.

They came to prominence as labor muscle field during the Cleaners and Dyers war, where the Purples and several Chicago hoods organized the Detroit Cleaners and Dyers by creating trade associations that they controlled and then extorted hundreds of thousands of dollars a year out of the industry, which was a lot of money in those days. The Purples' brutality in this is what helped them to make their mark in the underworld.

What distinguished the Purple gang from other gangs of the same size was their ready and willingness to kill. The gang, which never numbered more then 51 members, excelled in extortion, shipment protection, trafficking of narcotics, bootleg liquor, gambling and the occasional hijacking of unprotected liquor shipments.

In the mid-1920s, the Chicago mob under Al Capone made contacts with the gang. The Capone organization put the Purples in contact with their other satellite gang, Egan's rats out of St. Louis. Members of both gangs were suspected of taking part in the St. Valentines Days Massacre in Chicago.

Paul Kavief wrote;

"There was so much liquor coming through Detroit that Al Capone decided he was going to set up a base of operation here; well, in 1927 he came here and had a meeting with the Purples and the Italian mobs and told them what his idea was. Well, they told him, basically, "That river belongs to us" and that he wasn't moving in here. And Capone, who was an astute businessman, realized that instead of going to war with the Purples, it would just be easier set them up as his agents in Detroit. So the Purples put a label on Canadian Club whisky and called it Old Log Cabin, a really good quality liquor that they were selling to the Capone's."

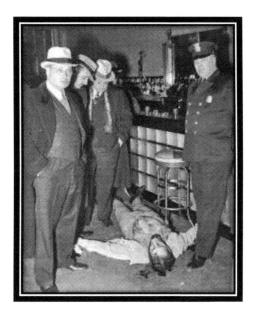

One of the people that Capone sold Old Log Cabin to was Bugs Moran. Bug Moran decided that he wasn't making enough money off his liquor sales and decided to buy from some hijackers who had an inferior product, which Moran was actually selling at a high profit. But, his distributors started complaining about the quality and when Moran called Capone and said that he wanted to start selling Old Log Cabin again, Capone said that he was sorry, that he had already sold Moran's consignment to somebody else.

So Moran started hijacking the Purple Gang supplied trucks, which probably brought the Purples in on the murder as conspirators. Three of the Purples rented rooms across the street from Moran's warehouse in fact and Abe Bernstein, acting as an anonymous hijacker, set up a deal with Moran to sell Moran a load of hijacked Purple gang liquor that he was willing to sell for a very low price and Moran agreed to meet him at his now famous garage.

The Purples acted as spotters, they watched the Moran's enter the garage and then tipped off a group of hitmen from a gang called Egan's Rats. Bugs Moran lived, because the Purples, not familiar with the Chicago underworld, mistook Al Wienshank as Moran."

In the late 1920s, The gang became so well known for kidnapping that they were, for a short time, prime suspects in the disappearance of the Lindburgh baby. Their nationwide reputation eventually did them in. Although the gang remained a force in the Underworld of prohibition, they started to fall apart in the early 1930s. The 1931 butchering of gangsters Hymie Paul, Izzy Sutker and Joe Leibovitz at 1740 Collingwood Avenue on September 16,1931 and the convictions that followed, signaled the end of the Purple Gang forever.

Ziggy Selbin and Irving Shapiro were killed in October 1929.Philip Keywell, was sentenced to life in prison in 1930 for murder. Morris Raider was sentenced to 12-15 years in prison in 1930 for murder. Raymond Bernstein, Harry Keywell and Irving Milberg were sentenced to life in prison in 1931 for murder. Abe Axler was killed in 1933, as was Eddie Fletcher. Harry Millman was killed in 1937. Harry Fleisher and Sam Fleisher were both sent to Alcatraz prison. The remaining members of the gang were eventually murdered or chased out of the underworld by the new mobs and by 1935, the Purple gang was no more. However, Abe Bernstein, one of the gang's leaders, continued to run bookmaking from his suite at the Book-Cadillac Hotel in Detroit until he died of a stroke in 1968.

The late Mr. Pullazi

Peter Pullazi, a collector on a Capone beer route, went into business for himself, so they syndicate killed him

Generic prohibition murders

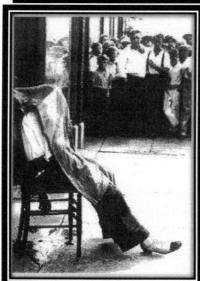

The late Mr. Provenzano

On December 10th 1969, in Palermo Italy, Bernardo Provenzano and his boys fell into a shot out with Michele Cavataio, boss of Acquasanta family and several of his men. Both Provenzano and a hood named Calogero were killed.

The late Mr. Quinlan

Walter Quinlan, a thug for hire, crawled out of Valley, Chicago's old Irish ghetto. His claim to fame was that he murdered Paddy "The Bear" Ryan, leader of the ruthless Valley gang. He was also one of the killers of Samoots Amatuna, a Genna family capo.

The late Mr. Reles

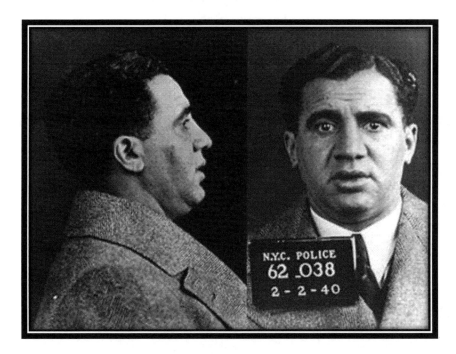

Abe Reles met his end at the Half Moon Hotel on the Coney Island Boardwalk. Located at West 29th Street and the Boardwalk, the spot where Henry Hudson was said to have landed. The name refers to explorer Henry Hudson's ship, which anchored off Gravesend Bay in Brooklyn (Coney Island), on its way to find to find a shorter route to Asia. A 16-story, 400-room hotel, $3 million hotel it was the pride of the boardwalk. Governor Al Smith spoke at the opening night of the hotel on Coney Island when it opened on May 5 of 1927 and the Ancient Order of Hibernians held their massive annual meeting in its conference rooms.

On November 12 1941, long after the Half Moon's glory days had passed, the New York City Police Department rented room 623 to hide away Abe Reles, a government witness against Murder Incorporated.

Surrounding Reles was a team of five New York City policemen including Detective Victor Robbins, James Boyle, John E. Moran, Frank Tempone and Harvey McLaughlin. All five were under the command of Captain Frank Bals.

In the underworld Reles, age 35, standing five foot four inches tall and under160 pounds, was considered weird and fanatical. Most reporters and policeman assumed he had a lower than normal IQ. The detectives later admitted that they despised Reles, who was arrested 44 times since the age of 13, and found him to be a filthy man with internal gastric problems that made being around him impossible. He was also surely and disliked the police. "All cops" he once said "are yellow and I'll fight anyone of them with guns, knife's or broken glass"

At 7:45 that morning, William Nicholson, who kept a private office on the second floor phoned the front desk to say to report a white sheet dangling down the side of the building. Reles, as police told it, had tried to climb out of the 6th floor window by tying a series of sheets together which broke causing him to plunge to the hotel concrete kitchen floor landing on his back and breaking his spine. Detectives swore that when they checked on Reles at 7:10 that he was sleeping, a radio on in the background.

Captain Bals later told the media...with a straight face...that it was his opinion that the detectives guarding Reles fell asleep. Reles decided to play a joke on them by slipping out the window, onto the roof and then walking back up to the room where the police were sleeping and knocking on the door to surprise them.

In 1963 federal witness Joe Valachi confirmed what virtually everyone in the United States assumed, that the police assigned to guard Reles had been paid off to toss him out the window. In 1954 the Metropolitan Jewish Geriatric Center converted the Half Moon to a nursing home and in the 1990s the building was finally demolished.

Frank Bals, long suspected as the payoff man behind the murder, was actually promoted after the Reles murder and retired from the force as a Deputy Police Commissioner. The promotion came in spite accusations by gangster harry Gross that he paid Bals for years to protect his gambling operations. But Bals was protected by District Attorney William O'Dwyer, Bals had been his chief investigator, who named Bals to the Deputy Commissioners spot after O'Dwyer became mayor.

Appearing before Kefauver Committee to explain Reles odd death, Bals claimed that all of the officers on duty must have been asleep when Reles climbed out the window. He could not, however, explain how Reles body flew fifty feet from the windows ledge before it hit the ground. Bals retired from the force and died in Florida in 1954 at age 62.

The case of Mr. Riesel

Abraham Telvi was a young punk from Brooklyn who was paid $1,175 (in two payments) by mobster Johnny Dio, to toss acid into the eyes of journalist Victor Riesel in front of Lindy's on Broadway on April 5, 1956. Riesel's offense was going after Dio in his column.

The attack left Riesel partially blind for the rest of his life. Some of the acid also splashed back on Telvi scarring his face and neck. The scars were so prominent that Telvi's brother Leo had to drive him to Youngstown Ohio to hide out for several weeks while the burns healed.

Although Telvi was arrested for the assault, police were unable to make the charges stick. Feeling safe from prosecution, Telvi then tried to extort more money from Dio, a fatal mistake. He was gunned down by persons unknown on July 28, 1956 at 282 Mulberry Street, on the Lower East Side, a bullet fired through the back of his head. He was 22 years old.

The late Mr. Riggiona

Louis Riggiona was another victim of New York mob justice. He was tracked down to the and shot twice through the heart by two gunmen as his left his clam bar on the east side. His brother Joe escaped. Of the six Riggiona brothers, in 1940, three were dead from gang violence and two were imprison for life.

The late Mr. Rosenheim

Julius Rosenheim, a member of the Capone organization, was discovered to be a police informer. He was dead before the end of the day, shot through the mouth.

The late Mr. Sabbatino

The bullet ridden chair of Sal Sabbatino, waterfront hiring boss who ran Sabbatino Co Inc, general stevedores. ILA Atlantic Coast district general vice president Emil Camarda was sitting here when on October 2, 1941 when he fell into an argument with Sabbatino, an associate of the Gambino crime family. Sabbatino shot Camarda six times. He was arrested and sent to Sing Sing prison for ten years. He did two and was released.

The late Mr. Sage

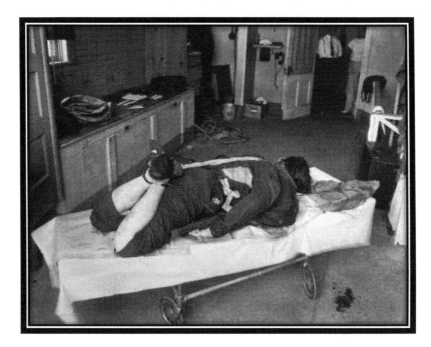

Walter Sage had been a member of Brooklyn's Abe Reles-Harry Maione wing of Murder Inc. when word got out that he might talk to the DA. He fled town but Pittsburg Phil Strauss tracked him down and stabbed him to death.

The late Mr. Schultz

In the fall of 1935, the new National Organized Crime Syndicate voted to kill Dutch Schultz. The Syndicate bosses felt that Schultz's time had passed, that he was an unstable relic from prohibition who had made several public statements that he intended to kill New York's popular District Attorney Thomas E. Dewey. The Syndicate handed the job to its enforcement arm, a group of Brooklyn based Jewish gangsters who had dubbed themselves "Murder Incorporated, who in turn handed the Schultz contract to Charles Workman, AKA "The Bug," "The Powerhouse," and "Handsome Charlie, crawled out of Manhattan's Lower East Side in 1908, one of seven children. His first arrested, of record anyway, came at age 18 for stealing a $12 bundle of cotton thread from a truck. A year later he was pinched again for shooting a man in a dispute over $20. The victim refused to Press charges, but Workman was sentenced to the New York State

Reformatory for violating parole in the cotton theft case. Over the next decade he would be locked up on a series of charges, most of them minor in nature and all of them violent.

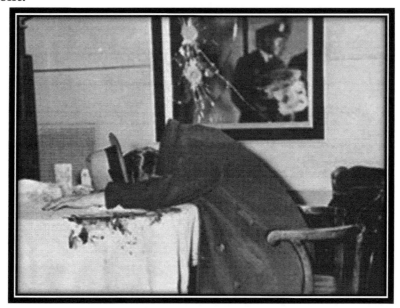

In the early 1930s, Workman became a gun-for-hire in the Brooklyn based Murder, Inc. for $125 a week. When bootlegger Dutch Schultz Threatened to murder New York's District Attorney Dewey, the Mafia ordered Murder Inc to take out Schultz.

Workman's partners on the hit were Murder, Inc. lieutenant Emmanuel "Mendy" Weiss, and a driver identified only by his nickname, "Piggy."
On the night of October 23, 1935, Workman walked into the Palace Chophouse in Newark, while Weiss provided cover outside although other put Weiss and Workman in the Barroom together.

Inside the bar Schultz sat with three of his man, Rosenkrantz, Landau and Berman.

The bartender on duty recalled that at about 10:15 "The front door opened suddenly and a heavy-set man walked into the barroom and I heard a voice order, 'Don't move, lay down.' I could hardly discern his face as he pulled his topcoat up to hide it. I saw him place his hand on his left shoulder and whip out a gun from a

holster. I didn't wait any longer. I dropped to the floor and lay behind the bar."
A second man entered behind him, who kept his overcoat drawn around him but not buttoned. They headed straight for the dining room.   Both gunmen, who knew Schultz by sight, saw that the Dutchman wasn't at the table. Schultz had put on his light topcoat and gray fedora and stepped into the men's room just seconds before the killers arrived.   One of the killers opened up on the three men at the table with a .38-caliber pistol just as the other gunman swept the table with the sawed-off shotgun he had brought in under his coat. It was over in seconds. Lulu Rosenkrantz managed to pull out a 45 but was quickly cut down Otto Berman, the oldest of the trio was hit six times.

 All the wounds--body, neck, wrist, elbow and shoulder were on the left side. Abe Landau was hit with a single shot that went through his left shoulder from the back. Another one went through the upper left arm and a third tore a gaping hole through his right wrist.   Two stray shots smashed the mirror. Four or five other bullets lodged in the walls.

  Schultz must have heard the shooting but stayed in the bathroom, he wasn't armed, except for a cheap 3-1/2-inch switchblade pocketknife. One of the gunmen kicked open the men's room door and got off a shot with that spare .45 he was carrying. The bullet struck Dutch in the just below the chest, on the left, and tore through the abdominal wall into the large intestine, gall bladder and liver before lodging on the floor near the urinal he had been using. A second bullet missed.

 The bartender recalled "The first thing I noticed was Schultz. He came reeling out like he was intoxicated. He had a hard time staying on his pins and he was hanging on to his side. He didn't say a cockeyed thing. He just went over to a table and put his left hand on it kind of to steady him and then he plopped into a chair, just like a souse would. His head bounced on the table and I thought that was the end of him but pretty soon he moved. He said, 'Get a doctor, quick,' but when he said it another guy gets off the floor (Rosenkrantz) He had blood all over his clothes but he gets up and he comes over to me and he looked like he was going to cry. He throws a quarter on the bar and he says, 'Give me change for that,' and I did."

Workman went through the Dutchman's pockets for cash and then ran out to the get- away car only to find out it was gone. His partners had left without him. Workman walked back to New York. Workman demanded that the mob give him Weiss's for abandoning him. A meeting was called with Lepke Buchalter who listened to both men pled their cases. Weiss won out with the reasonable argument that the shooting was business and robbing Schultz wasn't. He had warned Workman to leave and when he didn't, they left without him.

Inside the Palace Chop House on the night of the murders. This photo is taken from the rear of the restaurant looking out to the front door.

In 1940, Abe Reles, a mob informant, spilled the beans about Murder Inc. and Charlie Workman was quickly arrested and stood trial. Abe Reles, protected by a squad of New York City cops, was tossed out the window of his hotel room where he was being kept under the government protection as he testified against members of Murder Inc. Upon learning of Reles death, Lucky Luciano said "That bird could sing but he couldn't fly" The line was later used in the film On the Waterfront.

With the court and the case fixed against him, Workman pled no contest to the charges against him with the statement "I, Charles Workman, being of the opinion that any witness called in my defense will be intimidated and arrested by members of the District Attorney's office or police officials and not wishing members of my family and others to be subjected to humiliation on my account, do hereby order you as my counsel not to call any witnesses in my defense except myself. And I forbid you to call any other witnesses to the stand. "I further state if such witnesses are called I will openly state in court I do not want them to testify."

Workman was permitted a brief visit with his brother Abe, who threw his arms around him and wept uncontrollably. The Bug heard him give this advice "Whatever you do, live honestly. If you make 20 cents a day, make it do you. If you can't make an honest living, make the government support you. Keep away from the gangs and don't be a wise guy. Take care of Mama and Papa and watch 'Itchy' (a younger brother). He needs watching."

Workman was sent to Trenton State Prison. In 1942, he offered the Navy his services to go on a suicide mission against the Japanese Navy. The offer was declined.

In 1947 it was announced that he was dying from complications which had set in after an operation for gallstones. He was transferred to the Rahway State Prison Farm in 1952, and the question was asked, would a guy like that be safe in there? No problem. "Nobody is going to bother him in here," said Acting Superintendent Stephen Francsak. "It is just like on the outside. The men look up to a man with his background." He survived and worked in the prison commissary and Library and became a trusty.

He was a model prisoner, minding his own business, doing his work. He was denied parole in 1956. "If I had a thousand inmates like him I wouldn't have to worry with this job," said Warden Warren Pinto. "He's just like an ordinary guy, not one of the 'big shots' who try to gain special favors. He never asks for anything." The prison psychologist had Workman listed as "a reasonably stable individual   He was granted parole in 1964.

On his way to jail, Workman spoke to Stephen P. Flarity; a Newark News reporter.

"Charlie," Flarity said, "will you tell what you had intended to say if you took the witness stand?"

"Ask Kessler," Workman replied.

"Did Reles and Tannenbaum tell the truth on the witness stand?"

"Why not ask them?"

"Charlie, were you in Newark on the night of October 23, 1935?"

"Steve," Workman replied, "it's all over now. If you come to see me in 15 years I might talk to you."

But he never talked about any of the twenty murders including the Dutch Schultz murder.

As for Crazy Owney Madden, he retired from the rackets in the early 1930s, and moved to Hot Springs, Arkansas, a fast-developing tourist resort with a reputation for illegal gambling and a wide open policy on victimless crime. Owney of course, had some financial interests in a few casinos and once in while open his home to gangsters on the run from the law. Al Capone was an occasional guest as was Lucky Luciano.

Once, a deputy sheriff knocked on Madden's door in the middle of the day and announced that he had brought along some out of town visiting relatives who wanted to meet the gangster in the flesh. Owney was gracious and spent several minutes with the visitors. When they were about to leave, he pulled the deputy aside, and never losing the smile on his face whispered "You ever pull a stunt like that again and I'll ripe your heart out with a kitchen knife" Owney "Killer" Madden died in 1964 of natural causes in Hot Springs. He died peacefully and wealthy at the age of 72.

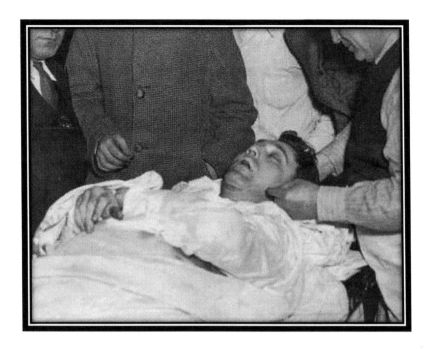

Schultz, still alive being carried into the hospital

The late Mr. Schuster

Albert Anastasia

Arnold L. Schuster was a longtime Brooklyn resident who recognized wanted bank robber Willie Sutton while riding on a New York subway in February 1952. Following Sutton to a garage, Schuster called the police of Sutton's whereabouts resulting in the robber's later arrest as Sutton was changing a dead battery from his car, which had stalled in the street.

Tenuto

After receiving a modest amount of publicity from New York City press, as well as appearing on the hit TV show I've Got a Secret], Schuster himself was murdered outside his home on March 8, 1952, shot twice in the groin and once in each eye.

Frederick J. Tenuto, a mob associate, was arrested for the crime but released. Several years later, government informant Joe Valachi claimed Albert Anastasia had ordered Schuster's death after witnessing one of his television interviews. Although Sutton had no connection with the Gambino crime family, Anastasia was reportedly angered by Schuster, stating, "I can't stand squealers! Hit that guy!" and Schuster was dead.

The late Mr. Siegel

Born in Brooklyn as Benjamin Hyman Seigel. One of five children of Austrian-Jewish immigrant parents. Siegel spoke German. Casino owner. Born Feburary 28, 1906. Died June 20, 1947. When the Gangster Chronicles came on television in the late 1970's, a relative of Bugsy Siegel remarked to Meyer Lansky, Siegel's lifelong business partner, that he was considering suing the production company for depicting Bugsy as an uncontrollable killer.

"What are you going to sue them for?" asked Lansky. "In real life he was worse."

Unlike most hoods who dominated gangdom in the 1930's, Siegel was smart and he knew it. He hated the poverty and ignorance of the world he was raised in and detested the illiterate and uncouth men he had to deal with. He wanted more, he wanted to be on the other side. In fact, Siegel wanted to be on the other side, the legitimate side, so badly, that he invested a million dollars in the stock market in 1933, but lost half of it when the market crashed in October. "If I had kept that million," he said, "I'd have been out of the rackets right now."

Siegel knew that if he stayed in New York, nothing would ever change, so he, and not the New York branch of the syndicate as is commonly reported, decided to try his luck out west in Los Angeles. He had been a regular visitor out there since 1933, introducing himself as an independent sportsman, a title that didn't fool anybody.

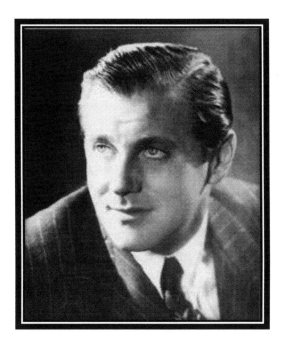

Of course, Bugsy had other motives. Gangsters always do. He had stabbed another hood in a dispute over a card game, cutting the man in the stomach 20 times to make sure gases would not allow his body to float to the surface, and now the cops wanted to talk to him about that. He had also been named in a scam to fix boxing matches and had ordered the killing of a bookie who had cheated him. When the bookie found out about the death order, he went to the cops and told them everything he knew, so for the time being it was best he went to the West Coast.

Siegel took over the Screen Extras Guild and the Los Angeles Teamsters, which he ran until his death. With control of the Screen Extras Guild, Siegel was able to shake down Warner Brothers Studios for $10,000, with a refusal to provide extras for any of their films. He also shook down his movie star friends for huge loans that he never paid back, and when he came back for another loan, he always got it, because they were, justifiably, terrified of him.

He once bragged to Lansky that he had fleeced the Hollywood crowd out of more than $400,000 within six months of his arrival. He was a one man terrorist campaign.

When Siegel arrived in LA, the number one racing service out west was James Ragen's Continental Press, which serviced thousands of bookies between Chicago to Los Angeles, each of whom paid Ragen between $100 to $1200. The owner, Jimmy Ragen, was a tough, two fisted, Chicago born Irishman, who had punched, stabbed, and shot his way to the top of the heap, without the Mob's help.

The Chicago outfit, then under Nitti, watched the money flood into Regan's office with envy. Nitti, and later Paul Ricca, tried to set up a rival service called Trans-American, with each mob boss across the country running the local outlet, doing whatever they had to do to take Ragen out of business.

In California, Siegel and Mafiosi Jack Dragna were charged with putting Trans-America in business and taking Ragen's Continental Press out of business. Eventually, the Chicago mob settled the entire issue by shooting Ragen as he drove his car down a Chicago street. Ragen survived the shooting, but not the dose of mercury a nurse working for the outfit shot up into his vein a few days later. With Ragen dead, Continental Racing Services was divided up among the various bosses who had helped to build it, and Jack Dragna was named to run the California office. Siegel was shocked. He had risked his life to build the service out west, he had worked on it day and night, at the least he expected to be cut in on perhaps half the franchise.

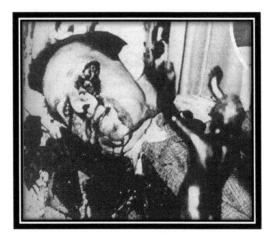

Instead, all he was got was a visit from Chicago's chief fixer, Murray Humphreys, who told Siegel to fold up Trans-America wire service. They didn't need it anymore. The syndicate owned Continental Press. But Siegel sent Humphreys packing with a message for Paul Ricca... if the Chicago people wanted Siegel to fold up Trans-America in Nevada, Arizona and Southern California, it would cost them $2,000,000 in cash.

Even though the Chicago outfit didn't want Siegel working for them, at the same time, they didn't want him working for New York either. Crazy or not, Siegel was smart, ambitious and ruthless. They had to watch him, so Paul Ricca told Charlie Fischetti, one of his most dependable torpedoes, to send out a spy, and the woman they chose was the same woman Bugsy Siegel came to call his Flamingo, Virginia Hill.

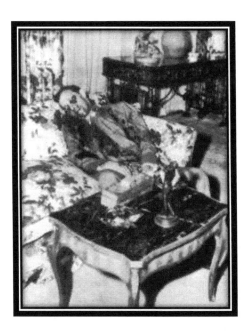

 Virginia Hill was a foul-mouthed, tough-talking product of the poverty of Bessemer, Alabama who came to Chicago when she was 17, to find work in the Century of Progress Exhibition of 1933. She worked at a variety of jobs across the city, including a stint as a shimmy dancer for $20 a week, but, finally ended up as a street hooker, turning tricks for as little as fifty cents or as much as five dollars, it depended on how desperate the John was.

Virginia eventually fell under the command of Charlie and Joe Fischetti, who were heading up the mob's prostitution rackets at the time. Virginia was, more or less, adopted by Jake Guzik and his wife, who offered to put her in charge of several brothels they still owned, but Virginia turned them down. She said she had higher aspirations. But what she did take from Guzik was an introduction to Joe Epstein, or Joey Epp, as he liked to be called, a mild-mannered, middle class, mob accountant who wore thick black glasses and barely spoke to those around him. Nevertheless, he was dependable and honest, by mob standards, and had been Guzik's understudy since 1930 and would one day be his second-in-command.

 Epp ran the outfit's racetracks with such authority the newspapers called him Illinois' unofficial racetrack commissioner. And while Epstein was well read, some said an intellectual, he loved to party and he was fascinated by the lowlife around him. He fell head over heels in love with Virginia Hill, and put her on the payroll as his mistress.

But it was a working relationship as well. Epstein put Virginia to work as a courier, bringing suitcases full of the mob's dirty money from Chicago, Kansas City, Cleveland and Los Angeles to syndicate owned and run banks in Cuba, Mexico, the Dominican Republic, France and Switzerland. There, the money was laundered, usually at a price of ten cents on a dollar and then invested in legitimate business from which the hoods could draw a salary.

The second part of the plan called for Virginia to get in touch with Bugsy Siegel, which she did, having met, and romanced him, several times in the past. Like Joey Epp before him, Bugsy Siegel fell head over heels in love with Virginia. He called her his "Flamingo" and drenched her in jewelry, furs and gowns.

Virginia reported every conversation she had with Siegel back to the Fischetti brothers in Chicago. Still, the boys back in Chicago never trusted Hill, or anyone else for that matter, and when Paul Ricca came to power, he told Johnny Roselli (1033 Wilshire Blvd. Los Angeles) to start an affair with Hill so he could keep tabs on her.

Then, Siegel watched a colorful Los Angeles hood named Tony Cornero move his entire gambling organization out of California and into Nevada where he and his brothers opened a rundown but very profitable casino on the Vegas Strip. Within a year, Siegel had the cash, most of it from the New York end of the syndicate, to build the fabulous Flamingo Hotel.

In May of 1947, one month before he was executed, Bugsy Siegel called Jimmy Fratianno, a Los Angeles hood who, technically anyway, worked for Chicago, and asked him to come out to Las Vegas for a meeting. He didn't tell them what it concerned, but, as they found out, it was a recruitment drive. He had already made the same pitch to Jack Dragna, Bugsy Siegel was planning the unheard of, he was going to start his own organization out in the Nevada desert.

Virginia Hill had already reported Siegel's plans to Paul Ricca in Chicago, and, even though the Chicago mob was chiseling Siegel in the Flamingo by sending in professional gamblers to break the bank, they were indignant. As far as they were concerned, although the syndicate had agreed to allow Vegas and Reno to operate as open cities, it was clearly understood in the syndicate that Chicago controlled everything west of the Mississippi.

Siegel was a regional problem at a time when the mob thought it had gotten over its regional misunderstandings. He was a relic from the past. He had to be removed.

On June 8, 1947, Virginia Hill got a call from Epstein back in Chicago, he told her to get out of town, to go to France, she could tell Siegel she was going there to buy wine for the casino as she had in the past. He wouldn't question that. Virginia knew, immediately, why she had to leave town. They were going to kill Bugsy and the boys back in Chicago didn't want their best cash courier and narcotics peddler splattered with blood and headlines. Virginia flew into Chicago and met Epstein at Midway airport, where he gave her $5,000 and then she continued to Paris.

Back on the West Coast, Bugsy Siegel, caught in the middle of an uprising, was too busy to care where Virginia was. Several days before, Siegel told Micky Cohen to tell all of the bookies in Los Angeles, Reno and Vegas that the price for using the wire service was going to double. But, to Siegel's amazement, the bookies refused to pay, they knew that Chicago was taking over and that they were planning to kill Siegel.

And, on June 20, 1947, that's what they did.

Jack Dragna gave the order to a hood named Frankie Carranzo. When the call came, Carranzo drove up to Beverly Hills and parked his car a few feet from Siegel's home, wound the silencer onto the barrel of his .30 caliber, army issue carbine, and walked around to the back of the house. He hid in the shadow of a rose-covered lattice work with his army carbine and released an entire clip into the living room through a 14-inch pane of glass.

Nine slugs in all. Two of them tore apart Bugsy's face as he sat on a chintz-covered couch. One bullet smashed the bridge of his nose and drove into his left eye. The eye was later found on the dining room floor, fifteen feet away from his dead body. The bullet was found in an English painting on the wall. The other entered his right cheek, passed through the back of his neck, and shattered a vertebra, ripped across the room.

At exactly 11:00 A.M., Jack Dragna got a call from Carranzo: "The insect was killed," and he then hung up.

A few minutes before that call, at 10:55, Little Moe Sedway and Gus Greenbaum, two hoods with gambling backgrounds, strode into the Flamingo and announced over the intercom system, "OK, we're taking over."

Everyone present knew who "we" were.

The only persons to attend Siegel's funeral services at Beth Olam Cemetery were his brother and a Rabbi.

The Flamingo's next manager was Gus Greenbaum. He did his job. The hotel was completed and enlarged from 97 to two hundred rooms. By the end of the year the casino posted a $4 million profit, $15 million before the skim, clearing the way for the skimming to begin.

Saint Valentine's Day Massacre

Saint Valentine's Day Massacre: There is no proof, but if legend is correct, the massacre of the infamous St. Valentine's Day Massacre was planned by Machine Gun Jack McGurn (Vincenzo Gibaldi) Several days before the murders, someone from the Capone organization.... someone whose voice Boss George Bugs Moran (1893-1957) would not recognize, placed a call to the Irishman, posing as an independent hijacker with a load of hijacked Old Log Cabin whiskey to sell at a below market price.

The scene of the massacre

Moran leaped at the offer. The caller said he would call back when he had the shipment ready. Two weeks passed before the Capone hood called Moran again. He said he had a shipment that he could deliver on February 14, 1929, Valentine's Day, at 11 a.m. Moran said he would be there with his crew to help unload the truck on the gang's garage on 2122 North Clark Street. Moran had called the gang the night before and told them to be at the garage early, he was expecting a shipment of Old Logan Cabin Whiskey between 10 and eleven o'clock Temperatures had dipped to zero that Thursday morning, February 14, 1929. The sky was gray and the streets were covered with a blanketed of snow and ice, causing a bad rush hour, worse than usual. More snow was predicted for the end of the day.

That morning, Al Capone was in Florida at his beachfront mansion. The first to arrive at the brick, one story warehouse of the S-M-C Cartage Company garage at 2122 North Clark Street was John May, who unlocked the front doors at about 8:30 a.m. He wanted to get an early start on a flatbed requiring a new oil pan. He brought with him his beloved Alastatian named Highball, who, from where he was leashed to the truck's gate. May, at 35, (1894-1929) was the least dangerous of the group. A $50 a week mechanic, May had joined up with the Moran's after a failed career as a safecracker. His one arrest, in 1913, for larceny, was stricken from the records.

The son of Irish immigrant parents, and the father of seven children, he had promised his wife, Hattie he would stay out of trouble and the day he left for the garage, he carried a case with a saint's medal in his back pocket. He was working on a truck that morning, with his dog tied to the bumper, while six other men waited for the truck of hijacked whiskey to arrive.

The always-miserable Gusenberg (Gusenberger) brothers arrived at about 9:30 they were the toughest members of the gang. Frank Gusenberg AKA Hock (1888-1929) was married to Lucille Gusenberg and Ruth Gusenberg at the same time. (Unknown to them)

The son of a German immigrant, Frank's first arrest came in 1911 (under the name Bloom) for disorderly conduct, although from 1909 to 1914 he was held as a suspect in numerous robberies and burglaries. In 1911, he served 90 days in the Bridewell prison for disorderly conduct. In 1924 he was tried, but found not guilty of burglary. Another robbery charge in 1926 was dismissed Peter Gusenberg ((1889-1929) AKA Goosey never explained to his wife Myrtle Coppleman, that he was a gangster. Instead, she was convinced that he was salesman whose last name was Gorman.

Peter Gusenberg appeared on police blotters in 1902 for larceny, did three years at Joliet prison for burglary in 1906 until 1909, but was returned there in 1911 on a parole violation. In 1923 he was sentenced, with Big Tim Murphy, to three years in Leavenworth on a mail robbery charge. Primarily, the Gusenberg's are enforcers for enforcers for Moran. James Clark (1887-1929) and Adam Heyer (1888-1929) followed the Gusenberg's into the garage.

Clark (Albert Kachellek) was 42 years old, the son of German immigrant parents. His record started in 1905 for confidence games and robbery, robbery in 1910 followed by a term in Pontiac reformatory for burglary. The States Attorney's struck two charges of robbery and one of murder from the records in

1914. Since he was constantly in trouble, he changed his name to James Clark for his mother's sake. Clark was primarily an enforcer.

Adam Heyer, age 40, AKA Adam Hayes, John Snyder, Frank Snyder was the Moran's business manager and accountant. The warehouse was leased in his name. Seven months before he had married his wife Mame. Heyer's record went back to 1908 for armed robbery, for which he served a year in the Bridewell prison. In 1915, he was sent to Joliet prison for running a confidence game. Released a year later, he was locked up again on a parole violation in 1923.

Albert Weinshank, (Weinshenker, 1903-1929) arrived last. The son of a Russian immigrant father, Weinshank was part of Moran's Cleaners and Dyers racket. Otherwise, he owned a speakeasy, the Alcazar. From a distance he bore a resemblance to Moran and the Capone look out's may have mistaken him for Moran on the day of the massacre.

The last to enter the garage was probably Dr. Reinhardt Schwimmer, age 29. (1900-1929) An optometrist. Not a gangster himself, Schwimmer is thrilled to be in the company of real gangsters. He had been around the gang since the days of Dion O'Bannion.

By 10:30 a.m., there were seven men gathered in the garage. As May worked on the truck, the others drank coffee and warmed themselves near a small iron space heater in the corner.

After Weinshank, the man who resembled Moran, entered the garage, two of Capone's lookout's who were stationed across the street on the third floor of a Mrs. Doody's boarding house, (2119 North Clark, still standing) picked up the phone and (probably) called the Circus Café where the killers were waiting in a rented garage at 1722 North Wood, and told them that Moran had arrived.

The four climbed into a black, 1927 Cadillac, doctored to look like a police car. Two of the assassins were dressed as police officers. The other three wore long trench coats and fedoras. Tucked inside their coats were sawed-off shotguns and Thompson submachine guns.

If Fred Killer Burke was there, he was probably driving the car, which pulled up outside the SMC Cartage Company a few minutes past 10:30. At the Parkway Hotel, several blocks away from the garage, George Bugs Moran kissed his wife Alice goodbye and took the elevator down to the lobby where he met Ted Newberry waiting. Moran was late getting up that morning. It was already 10:30

As he and Newberry were rounding the corner, they spotted the police wagon rolled up. Figuring the police were there for just a routine bust, Moran and Newberry took a left from the alley they were walking on to Clark Street from and had a coffee until the raid was over.

At about that same moment, another Moran enforcer, Willie Marks, was approaching the garage from a different angle, spotted the police, and also veered off the path. After a re-enactment of the crime, authorities concluded that the two men dressed as policemen entered the garage and acted as if they were police on a routine investigation. They disarmed the Moran's and forced them up against the wall.

As soon as their backs were turned, the two men in plain clothes entered with rifles and machine guns and shot them down. A bullet struck the small metal case that mechanic John May was carrying in his back pocket. Half of May's face was obliterated by close up shotgun blast.

Witness saw the two uniformed policemen exit the garage while escorting two plain clothed men who held their hands up in the air, as if they were under arrest. May's dog, inside of the warehouse, was barking and howling and when neighbors went to check and see what was going on… they discovered the murder scene. When the police arrived, they found Frank Gusenberg alive, breathing heavily and choking on his own blood. When he was asked for the identity of the killer, he shook his head "No" and breathed, "I'm not going to talk," before he laid his head back and died.

When a rumor spread that it was actually Chicago policemen, and not gangsters dressed as policemen, who did the killing, a forensic scientist from New York, Calvin Goddard, was called in to test all the machine guns in the police forces possession to rule out the possibility.

Goddard could not match up any weapon in the police arsenal to the bullets found at the scene. Some think that two of the killers, the two dressed as policemen, were Capone killers John Scalise and Albert Anselmi, who had been used in

Almost every Capone hit of any importance during the Twenties. Other suspects, Louis Campagna, (1900-1955) Claude "Screwy" Maddox, a member of the Circus Gang, Joey Lolordo, younger brother of the murdered Pasquelino, Tony Accardo, Sam Giancana, Machine Gun McGurn, George 'Shotgun' Ziegler, and (1897-1934) Gus Winkler and 'Crane Neck' Nugent No one will ever know with exact certainty that the killers were.

The only person closely identified was Fred "Killer" Burke also known as Fred Dane. Machine guns found in his home were tested and compared to bullets removed from the dead gangsters and were perfect matches. A woman who noticed the killers flee also described Burke. She identified Burke as the policeman who was wearing round sunglasses and missing tooth. Burke was never brought to Illinois to be tried for the massacre. Instead he was convicted for the killing of a policeman in Michigan and sentenced to life.

Willie Marks was lucky that day. He cheated fate, but fate caught up with him in the summer of 1933, when, acting as a bodyguard for Chicago's Teamster President Pat Burrell, he and Burrell were murdered by the Mob as they fished in a Wisconsin Lake. Several months later, the Mob caught up with Teddy Newberry too. His sin was to take a stab at power in an ill-fated partnership with Chicago's Mayor Anton Cermak.

In the middle of the day, the Boys yanked Newberry off of a Northside Street, pulled him into the back seat of car, tied him in barbed wire, beat him savagely, burned his face with cigarettes and finally shot him through the head and dumped in road side ditch in Indiana.

By November of 1946, Bugs Moran had fallen on hard times and had turned to pulling off small time robberies. By 1947, the Bugs were serving twenty to life behind bars for a bank robbery in Ansonia, Ohio. He died in a prison hospital, of lung cancer, in February of 1957. The Moran gang executioners didn't fare much better.

A hustler named Jimmy "Bozo" Shupe who provided the guns used in the massacre, was stabbed to death. Joe Giunta, John Scalise and Albert Anselmi, all suspected gunman in the massacre, were dead by 1934, all murdered by the Mob. Al Capone beat the later two to death with a baseball bat. The Purple Gang, who arranged the fake whisky shipment to bring the gang to the garage, and may have provided the look outs as well, were killed off before the close of the decade, mostly at their own hands. Right after the massacre, police raided the home of Fred "The Killer" Burke, a member of the Egan's Rats gang, where they found the Tommy Guns used in the massacre. Burke fled Chicago to Michigan, where he shot and killed a patrolman named Charlie Skelly three times, after Skelly tried to stop Burke for his part in a hit and accident.

The Skelly murder outraged the state of Michigan, and when Burke was finally captured a year later, it refused to honor Chicago's request to extradite the killer to face trial for his role in the St. Valentine's Day Massacre. Burke died in the Michigan State prison and never talked about the Valentine's Day killings. However, according to a jailhouse snitch, Burke's playmates in the massacre included "Smiling" Gus Winkler and Murray Humphreys. In late 1933, Winkler was murdered outside of a beer plant, owned by Cook County Commissioner Charles Weber, at 1414 Roscoe Street. As Winkler strolled towards Weber's office, the killers leaped out of a green truck and fired low, into his waist.

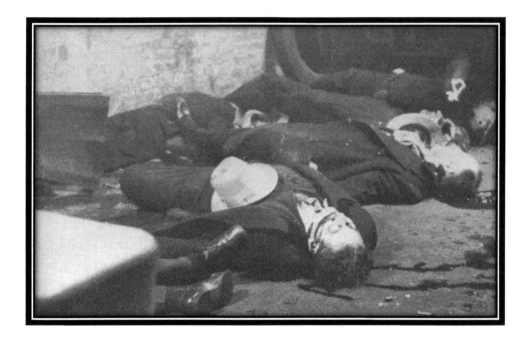

In all, 72 pellets and bullets went into Winkler in a matter of seconds; he was literally riddled with gunshot from his neck to his ankles. It was never clearly established why Winkler was killed or who killed him. It could have been anyone, for any one of a hundred reasons.

By 1933, Machine Gun Jack McGurn, the number one suspect in the massacre, was broke and out of power. How broke McGurn was came through when newspaper reporters found him in a midtown restaurant and asked him if he had anything to do with the kidnapping of Jake the Barbers son, Jerome Factor.

"Boys" McGurn said "I ain't made a payment on my house, the roof over my head, in 11 months, so's I guess I'm gonna lose the place to foreclosure. So if I snatched Jake's kid, believe you me, I would have collected the dough long before this"

Three years later, Jack McGurn went down to Florida and begged Willie Heeney, a pimp and drug addict under Capone, but a power in the labor extortion business, to set up a meeting between him, the Mobs banker, Jake Guzak and Nitti. In the old days, Heeney would have told the world that one of Capone's top sluggers was interested in talking to him.

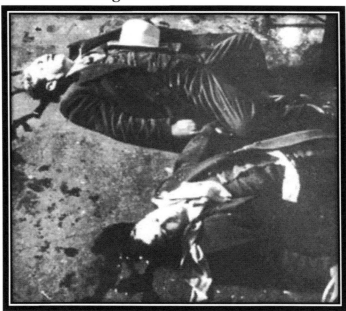

Now it was different. At the age of 33 McGurn's world had fallen apart. The Saint Valentine's Day murders had made him too hot for the syndicate to deal with. His gorgeous wife, Louis, "The Blonde Alibi" he had used to keep him from being convicted for his role in the Massacre by testifying they were holed up in a love nest at the time of the shooting, left him years ago when his money ran because of his gambling problem.

Now McGurn was reduced to running numbers and selling junk, dope, in the Black neighborhoods. But he wasn't much good at that either. McGurn was never an "earner", a money hustler; he was an enforcer, a pretty boy killer, with a mean streak. But, with Capone gone and the beer wars over, McGurn was of no use to anyone anymore. And a lot of hatred towards him from inside the Mob was personal.

As McGurn went down the in the ranks, the hoods that had been on the lower end of the chain, like Heeney, were rising up and they delighted in abusing the once arrogant McGurn, now that Capone wasn't around to protect him. Now, in 1936, when the Mob was on the brink of earning more money than it ever dreamed of, Machine Gun Jack McGurn had to beg for a five-minute appointment to see Heeney, Guzak and Nitti. In the meeting, held on a golf course outside Miami, McGurn said that he needed a job inside Nitti's loan sharking operation. They turned him down. He was high profile and the stigma of the massacre never left him. In desperation, McGurn launched into a plan he had of running dope from the Caribbean into Chicago to flood the Black neighborhoods. If the bosses would front the money, McGurn swore, his plan would make them all rich.

That's how far down the ladder McGurn was. He didn't know Nitti was already working with Lucky Luciano to establish dope routes in California and Florida. McGurn was dismissed and told to return to Chicago. He was all done in the rackets as far as they were concerned.

In 1936, the evening before Saint Valentine's Day, Machine Gun Jack McGurn went bowling at a second floor alley at 805 Milwaukee Avenue. (Still standing, it has been a warehouse for many decades since the murder) Three men walked in and stood behind his chair. One of them said "Stick em up and stand where you are." Nobody knows who the three men were.

Years later, Tony Accardo said he had been in the group, but as Accardo's power grew, and fewer and fewer people questioned his tales, The Accardo had a tendency to put himself virtually everywhere in Mob history including his claim that he was one of the gunmen at the massacre. While that doesn't seem likely, there is some evidence that Accardo and other member of his Alma Mata, the Circus Gang, did plan the massacre. One of the three killers whispered to McGurn "This is for you, you son a bitch" and then aimed a pistol carefully just below McGurn's right ear, and then fired a volley into the McGurn. Then he fired another round into his lower neck.

The pool hall owner, oddly enough named Tony Accardo, watched the first bullet enter McGurn, and then leaped for the floor and rolled under a pool table, and then watched the men carefully stretch out McGurn's body on the alley way and leave a card on his chest that showed a man and women without clothes on, staring at a sign that read "House for sale."

The card read
"You lost your job"
"You lost your dough
"Your Jewels and Handsome Houses"
"But things could be much worse you know"
"You could have lost your trousers"

Before the killers left, one of them turned and walked back to the table where McGurn had been sitting just a minute before, and took the tally sheet which had the names of McGurn's bowling partners on it, shoved it in his pocket and walked away into the night. The police found $3.85 in his pockets. There was no life insurance policy, but somehow the family managed to have him buried in a $1,000.00 copper coffin. His three younger brothers carried him to his grave, while McGurn's mother wailed "Why! Why did they kill my boy? He never did anything to anybody!"

Al Capone, jailed at Alcatraz, sent a dozen white roses. Sixteen days later, on March 2, perhaps remembering the families tradition for vengeance, the Mob hunted down McGurn's younger brother and former bodyguard, Anthony, to a local pool hall where he was playing cards and cut him to pieces with a rifle. Nobody will ever know who killed McGurn or why. The popular theory was that Bugs Moran had done the deed, but that doesn't seem likely.

In June of 1958, Claude Maddox died in his sleep, of natural causes. Maddox had been the boss of the Old Circus gang, and had played a major role in planning the massacre by providing the guns, police car and uniforms. Unlike everyone else connected to the murders, Maddox had played his cards right over the years, and rose up in syndicate, working under Jake Guzak for a while, and then for Murray Humphreys. He died a rich, powerful man. It was Maddox who burned and chopped up the car used to carry the killers to Moran's warehouse, and if the testimony of a hood named Byron Bolton is to be believed, Maddox was also one of the murders at the massacre, although that seems doubtful. The FBI showed up to photograph Maddox's funeral, and the burial. Tension was high and several hoods in attendance talked about shooting the agents until Boss Tony Accardo's cooler head prevailed.

The other primary killers in the massacre were the Purple Gang of Detroit. The gangs undisputed leader was Sammy "Purple" Cohen who joined his gang with the Oakland Sugarhouse gang under the direction of the Bernstein brothers, Abe, Ray and Joe. Together they were transformed from a small time gang of troublesome teens to bootleggers and occasional muscle for other, larger bootleg gangs. Author Paul Kavieff, who has written extensively about the gang said "The Purples were, for the most part, the sons of recently immigrated Russian Jews, although some of the members were actually born in the old country and brought here as infants, all of them were the sons of the working poor. The Purples were really a very loose confederation of mostly, but not exclusively, Jewish gangsters. Well, the gang started as a group of juvenile delinquents on the lower east side of Detroit, a group of about 16 or 17 children from the same neighborhood. Mostly they were involved in the usual petty crime of juveniles, rolling drunks and stealing from hucksters. It was the advent of prohibition that really got them organized, prohibition started in Michigan on May 1, 1918. Detroit was really the first US City with a population of over 250,000 to have a prohibition law. The opportunities provided by that, early prohibition, are what helped to escalate these kids into mobsters. Remember, Detroit is a mile away from Windsor, Canada and beer was easily available there from their export docks. Strangely, Ontario, where Windsor is, had a prohibition law but not a law against exporting liquor to countries that didn't have prohibition, so just about anybody with a rowboat could go over there, and tell the export people they were picking up a shipment that was to go to Cuba. Nobody asked a lot of questions. The money was fantastic, by 1923 the bootleg business in Detroit was estimated to be over $250,000,000 a year, but the Purples weren't so much involved in bootlegging liquor as they were hijacking liquor and that was really how they made their reputation. They were a predatory group and they were known for their ruthlessness, I mean they shoot everybody during these hijackings, even the guys who were simply driving the trucks.

What resulted was that if you were making a beer delivery and were robbed by the Purples, you fought to the death, because you knew that the Purples were going to haul you out of the truck and kill you anyway. By 1925, the Purples had established themselves as strong-arm guys, bodyguards and the like, for gamblers in Detroit. But what gave them life as a gang was that they had an enormous payroll, they had cops on their payroll, city officials, newspaper people, really they could not have operated the way they did without the official nod."

As to the gangs name, Kavieff wrote "There isn't a lot of available to clearly explain the origins of the name, but it was probably a journalistic adventure because I found no reference to any operation called the Purple Gang until 1928. One story was that when they were kids and were stealing from shopkeepers, one of the shopkeepers said that "those kids are off-colored, they're purple, purple like the color of bad meat." Another story is that there had been two brothers, Sam and Ben Purple, who had been associated with the gang when they were juveniles, but had nothing to do with the adult organized crime group. But I don't believe that has anything to do with it. Again, my best guess is that the name was a media invention.

The core group of the gang was composed of the Bernstein brothers, Abe and Joe, who were the leaders of the gang. Abe was more or less the diplomat Joe was the mover and shaker on the street.   He later became a legitimate businessman. The core was ten or twelve guys who grew up on the lower east side of Detroit. Sometimes the gang numbered as high as eighteen or slightly more.

The Purples did sell drugs, actually I should say, what they did was to create a protection racket for the hoods who did sell drugs as a main source of income. So a dealer could operate in the city and make a lot of money selling drugs in so long as they kicked back to the Purple Gang, if they didn't kick back to the Purples, then the Purples brutally put them out of business.   The same was true for the Handbook industry. Once there was one Handbook operator who refused to pay the Purples so they took him and brought him out to the Lake, cut a hole in it and dunked him in the ice a couple of times, after that, he paid.

The so-called Little Jewish Navy was a fraction of the Purple Gang and was led by a guy named One Armed Gelfin. Gelfin and several others in the group were Chicago gangsters who were thrown out of Chicago by the Capone mob, were the core of the group. Again, there were about ten or twelve members in all.   They were bankrolled in this venture by the Purples. The group also did enforcement work for the Purples too. Otherwise, they had about a dozen fast boats and they hauled liquor from Canada into Detroit.

They came to prominence as labor muscle field during the Cleaners and Dyers war, where the Purples and several Chicago hoods organized the Detroit Cleaners and Dyers by creating trade associations that they controlled and then extorted hundreds of thousands of dollars a year out of the industry, which was a lot of money in those days. The Purples' brutality in this is what helped them to make their mark in the underworld.

What distinguished the Purple gang from other gangs of the same size was their ready and willingness to kill. The gang, which never numbered more than 51 members, excelled in extortion, shipment protection, trafficking of narcotics, bootleg liquor, gambling and the occasional hijacking of unprotected liquor shipments. In the mid- 1920s, the Chicago mob under Al Capone made contacts with the gang.

  The Capone organization put the Purples in contact with their other satellite gang, Egan's rats out of St. Louis. "There was so much liquor coming through Detroit" Kavieff said "that Al Capone decided he was going to set up a base of operation here; well, in 1927 he came here and had a meeting with the Purples and the Italian mobs and told them what his idea was. Well, they told him, basically, "That river belongs to us" and that he wasn't moving in here. And Capone, who was an astute businessman, realized that instead of going to war with the Purples, it would just be easier set them up as his agents in Detroit. So the Purples put a label on Canadian Club whisky and called it Old Log Cabin, good quality liquor that they were selling to the Capone's.

One of the people that Capone sold Old Log Cabin to was Bugs Moran. Bug Moran decided that he wasn't making enough money off his liquor sales and decided to buy from some hijackers who had an inferior product which Moran was actually selling at a high profit, but his distributors started complaining about the quality and when Moran called Capone and said that he wanted to start selling Old Log Cabin again, Capone said that he was sorry, that he had already sold Moran's consignment to somebody else. So Moran started hijacking the Purple Gang supplied trucks, which probably brought the Purples in on the murder as conspirators.

Three of the Purples rented rooms across the street from Moran's warehouse in fact and Abe Bernstein, acting as an anonymous hijacker, set up a deal with Moran to sell Moran a load of hijacked Purple gang liquor that he was willing to sell for a very low price and Moran agreed to meet him at his now famous garage. The role of the Purples were the spotters, they watched the Moran's enter the garage and then tipped off a group of hitmen from a gang called Egan's Rats. That was why Moran lived, the Purples mistook Al Wienshank as Moran.

 The gang became so well known for kidnapping that they were, for a short time, prime suspects in the disappearance of the Lindbergh baby. Their nationwide reputation eventually did them in. Although the gang remained a force in the Underworld of prohibition, they started to fall apart in the early 1930s.The 1931 butchering of gangsters Hymie Paul, Izzy Sutker and Joe Leibovitz at 1740 Collingwood Avenue on September 16,1931 and the convictions that followed, signaled the end of the Purple Gang forever.

The remaining members of the gang were eventually murdered or chased out of the underworld by the new mobs and by 1935, the Purple gang was no more. The scene of the crime, Moran's warehouse, has its own dreary history as well.

In 1936, The S. M. C. Cartage Company, the site of the St. Valentine's Day murders, was an empty warehouse. No one wanted to buy it. That changed in 1945, when the Werner family turned it into an antique shop and were besieged by mail and visitors, crime buffs, from all over the world. The property was demolished in 1967, but a businessman named George Patey purchased the bricks from the infamous wall, and reconstructed them inside a bar room in Vancouver, Canada.

In 1997, the bricks were packaged individually and are now for sale over the Internet. Today, the murder site is a small, pleasant park for senior citizens, nothing else remains of it

The late Mr. Tancl

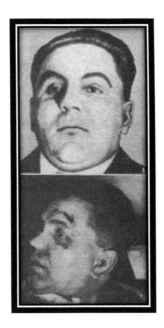

Tancl, alive (above) and dead (Below)

November 23, 1924, Myles O'Donnell and James Doherty enter the Hawthorne Inn Park that belonged to Eddie Tancl, a former prize fighter who refused to carry the O'Donnell Brothers beer. They drank some and left with some women but returned at about 6:00 AM and found Eddie Tancl, his wife, Leo Klimas and Mayme McClain seated together at a table. Doherty and O'Donnell joined them at the table. They had several drinks but refused to pay the bill. Suddenly, the thugs pulled their pistols and fired. Tancl made a try for his own gun, a .25 caliber gold plated and pearl handled German automatic, but the gun jammed and the bullets struck him down. Roman Hampe,l the bartender, threw a .38 in Tancl's direction while O'Donnell and Doherty ran for the door. Tancl followed, firing as he ran until he caught up with O'Donnell under a railroad pass where both men emptied their guns and fell. Tancl hit O'Donnell with the butt of the revolver before handing it over to waiter Martin Simet who had run out to join his boss. Tancl's last words to Simet were "kill him, he got me." And then he died.

The late Mr. Terranova

Italian judge Cesare Terranova was murdered in Palermo on September 25th 1979, killed him with him was his bodyguard policeman Lenin Mancuso. Terranova was murdered because of his constant investigations of the Mafia.

The late Mr. Treca

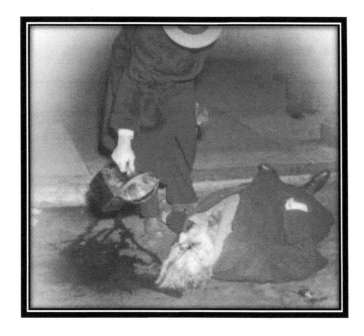

New York mob boss Vito Genovese was all about doing favors for powerful people so when Italian dictator Benito Mussolini wanted newspaper New York based Italian publisher Carlo Tresca was murdered, Vito carried it out. On January 11, 1943, one of Genovese's men gunned the newspaper man down in the streets with two shots through the head.

The late Mr. Van Meter

Homer Van Meter was a bank robber in the early 20th century and a criminal associate of John Dillinger and Baby Face Nelson. On August 23, at the corner of Marion Street and University Avenue in St. Paul, Van Meter was confronted by heavily armed four cops that included Chief of Police Frank Cullen, former chief Thomas Brown and two detectives.

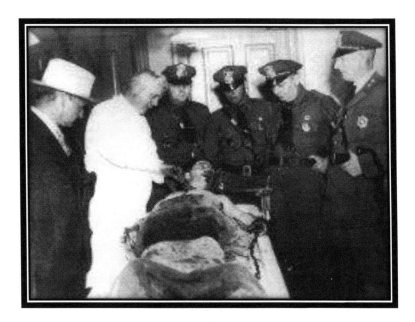

The cops say that Van Meter ignored their command to stop and fled into a nearby alley, where he opened fire on them. The cops returned fire and a dozen bullets ended the short life...he was 27 years old.... of Homer Van Meter. The number and severity of Van Meter's wounds—he was shot dozens of times, and several of his fingers were shot off—would cause some to label the incident an "ambush" or an example of "police execution". Van Meter's family would later say their kin had been used for "target practice".

The late Mr. Weiss

Hymie Weiss was boss of the Prohibition-era Chicago's North Side Gang and a bitter rival of Al Capone. On October 11, 1926, Weiss and four of his men (bodyguard Sam Pellar, gangster Paddy Murray, attorney William W. O'Brien, and Benjamin Jacobs, O'Brien's private detective.

The killers look- out point

At 4:00 that afternoon, the group was headed for the gang's headquarters, the old Schofield flower shop. As they rounded the corner to cross State Street, two gunmen hidden in a nearby rooming house opened fire with a submachine gun and shotgun. Weiss and Paddy Murray were fatally wounded by the first, very long burst. O'Brien was hit four times and staggered into a nearby stairwell.

Where the shots were fired from

Sam Pellar drew his .38 and fired a shot in the general direction of shooters but the bullet unintentionally struck Weiss as he collapsed onto the sidewalk. Pellar and Ben Jacobs, both wounded, staggered back the way they had come.

Bullets followed them the whole way and some chipped the cornerstone of the Holy Name Cathedral directly across the street. Many years later when the cornerstone was fixed and the bullet fragments removed, Chicagoans called it "The work of vandals"

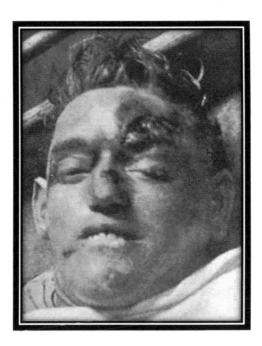

Weiss dead

The Weiss funeral

The late Mr. Yale

By 1927, Frankie Yale was one of the most powerful gangsters in Brooklyn and his long term partnership with Al Capone began to fray. The problem started when Capone's whisky started to disappear. As a major importer of Canadian whiskey, Yale supplied much of Capone's whiskey and was paid to oversee the safe arrival of the product to Chicago. However Yale started hijacking the truck before they left Brooklyn and blaming the raids on independent Irish gangsters.

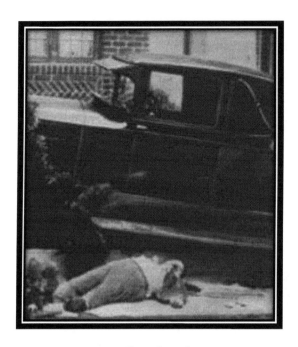

Yale, dead

Suspecting a double cross, Capone asked James "Filesy" DeAmato to keep an eye on his trucks. DeAmato reported back that Yale was hijacking his booze. Soon after this, Deamato realized that his cover had been blown and tried unsuccessfully to shoot Yale on July 1, 1927. Six nights later, DeAmato was gunned down on a Brooklyn street corner.

Yale's funeral

On Sunday afternoon, July 1, 1928, Yale was in his Sunrise Club, located at 14th Avenue and 65th Street, when he received a cryptic phone call. The caller said something was wrong with Yale's new wife Lucy, who was at home looking after their year-old daughter. Refusing Joseph Piraino's offer to drive him, Yale dashed out to his brand new, coffee-colored Lincoln coupe and took off up New Utrecht Avenue. At a red light, Frankie saw four hard-eyed men in a Buick sedan staring at him. While Yale's new Lincoln was fashioned with armor plating, the dealer had neglected to bullet-proof the windows. As a result, when the light changed, Yale hit the gas and took off. After a chase up New Utrecht, Frankie swerved west onto 44th Street, with the Buick close behind. Frankie's car was soon overtaken by the Buick, whose occupants riddled the Brooklyn gang boss with buckshot and submachine gun bullets. Yale's now out-of-control crashed into the stoop of a brownstone at No. 923.

The late Mr. Zuta

Jack Zuta was born Feburary 18, 1888 in Poland. Arrived in the US in 1913. Died August 1, 1930. A junk dealer by trade, Zuta drifted into crime as a teenager and eventually opened a string of brothels in commercial properties he owned on the West Side near Madison. However, he was driven out of business by Mike 'The Pike' Heitler and the Guzik Brothers. Zuta eventually moved to the west side and dabbled in gambling before returning to prostitution, this time with the protection of the Capone operation but in the mid-1920s, Zuta foolishly threw in with George 'Bugs' Moran and his North Side gang of misfits. When Moran went to war with Capone, Zuta threw his political and financial backing behind Moran.

Around the underworld, Zuta was widely disliked because of his incessant complaining and generally condescending and arrogant ways. Gangster considered him a coward and it was assumed that if and when Zuta was pinned by the law, that he would turn states evidence to save himself. However, the hoods also realized that he was a capable business executive with enormous police and political influence. (He wiretapped conversations and used them to blackmail his victims)

The Hotel Sherman Peace Treaty, reached by smaller outfit and the Capone organized on October 20, 1926, placed Zuta, Billy Skidmore, and Barney Bertsche, and their rackets were placed under the influence of the massive Capone operation. However, Zuta, like most of the North Side operators, despised Capone. Zuta was quick to conspire with the Moran and Aiello operations to kill Capone and take over his gang. On September 7, 1928, Antonio Lombardo, Capone's handpicked president of the powerful Unione Siciliano, and a bodyguard, were murdered by assassins near the corner of Dearborn and Madison. Zuta, and Joe and Dominick Aiello were arrested for suspicion in the murders and then released. Capone swore vengeance, making Zuta, essentially, a dead man.

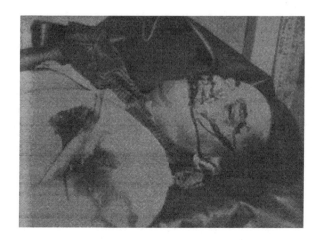

In June of 1930, Zuta is said to have put out a contract on the life of Jake Lingle, a reporter for the Chicago Examiner who was using his friendship with the chief of police and his position as a legman for the newspapers to extort money from the underworld. It happened that Zuta and his partners opened a massive gambling casino called the Sheriden Wave Tournament Club, which was closed by police after the outrage that followed the St. Valentine's Day Massacre. A year later, when things had cooled off considerably, Zuta was ready to reopen the club and Lingle was demanding $15,000 not to cause problems with the reopening. Zuta refused to pay and Lingle warned him, "If this joint is opened up, you'll get see more squad cars in front ready to raid it than you ever saw in your life before."

Zuta probably arranged for a North Side gangster named Frankie Foster to murder Lingle. The Lingle killing caused an uproar in Chicago and made international headlines. The Tribune newspaper offered a $55,000 reward for information and the federal government threatened to take over the investigation. Zuta, of course, was a prime suspect behind the murder, and on June 30, was hauled into police headquarters for question. With him was Leona Bernstein, Zuta's female friend and two business associates, Albert Bratz (AKA Eli Zoota, Jake Zuta's cousin) and Solly Vision. Released the next morning, July 1, at 10:30, Zuta and the others were released but Zuta seemed suddenly terrified to leave the station. Something or someone had scared him. He spotted Lieutenant George Barker, who was going off duty. According to Barker, Zuta approached him and said, "I'll be killed if I go through the loop. When you arrested me you took me from a place of safety and you ought to return me to a place of safety."

"I told him to run along" Barker said "and then he pleaded with me to help him for the sake of the woman with him. I finally told him I was driving to the loop and I would see him safely that far and he could get a cab downtown." As they drove along, Zuta cried out "We're being followed." Then a dark blue Chrysler with three men inside pulled up along Barker's car. A man in a tan suit wearing a Panama hat climbed out on the running board of the blue Chrysler, pulled out a .45 and fired seven shots into the car. Barker stopped the car, drew his service revolver and fired on the men in Chrysler who were now firing back at Barker. A stray bullet killed one bystander, a father of three children and injured a second. The gunmen broke off the battle when a patrolman arrived on the scene. Barker and the uniformed cop followed in Barker's car but near Adams Street, the Chrysler unleashed a cloud of gray smoke that created a large enough screen for the gunmen to escape. Barker was suspended for driving Zuta but later exonerated at a departmental hearing.

As for Zuta, he fled to the resort area in Waukesha County, Wisconsin, near Milwaukee. He had been there a month, living under the name J.H. Goodman, when he ran into Tony Scaler, a Milwaukee speakeasy owner who knew Zuta from Chicago. It was probably Scaler who told the Capone's where they find Zuta. On August 1, 1930 Zuta was overheard on a drug store pay phone saying to someone on the other end of the line "You better send someone up here damn quick. I want a bodyguard and an escort back to Chicago, and you better send 'em here in a hell of a hurry." Later, Zuta was in the dance pavilion of the Lake View hotel on Upper Nemahbin Lake near Delafield, Wisconsin. He was dropping coins in the player piano and while the tune "It May Be Good for You but it's So Bad for Me," was playing eight men with pistol and rifles surrounded Zuta and shot him 15 times. He was dead within minutes of hitting the floor. A meticulous record keeper, when police opened safe deposit boxes under his name, they found a slew of information on graft paid out to a series of Chicago public officials including a state senator, the Evanston Illinois chief of police and a Chicago Alderman. The $1,900 found in Zuta's pockets was taken by Internal Revenue agents who were looking into his income taxes.

Random Mob Hits through the Years

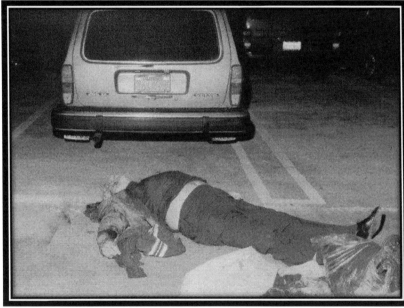

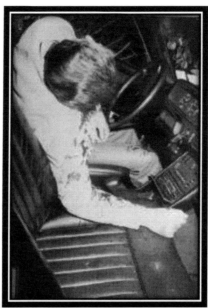

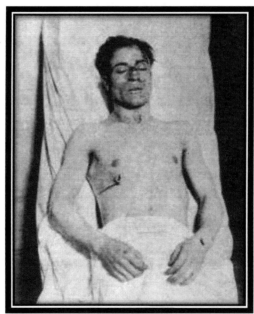

Made in the USA
Middletown, DE
26 October 2017